WHY PEOPLE BUY

MOTIVATION RESEARCH
and its
SUCCESSFUL APPLICATION

'You Call It Advertising, I Call It Indirect Aggression'

WHY PEOPLE BUY

MOTIVATION RESEARCH
and its
SUCCESSFUL APPLICATION

LOUIS CHESKIN
DIRECTOR, COLOR RESEARCH INSTITUTE PRESIDENT, LOUIS
CHESKIN ASSOCIATES, MARKETING RESEARCH

With an introduction by
Dr. Howard D. Hadley
RESEARCH VICE PRESIDENT, THE BUREAU OF ADVERTISING,
AMERICAN NEWSPAPER PUBLISHERS ASSOCIATION

tg
PUBLISHING
NEW YORK, NY

Printed in the United States
Reissue Edition

Please direct inquiries to:

Ig Publishing
Box 2547
New York, NY 10163
www.igpub.com

ISBN: 978-1-63246-032-5

I dedicate this book to
Charles W. H. Matthaxi
the man who has to make marketing decisions

CONTENTS

> We were trying to measure attitudes toward adult education, attitudes toward citizenship, social studies, traditional art and modern art.

> In the field of predetermining how consumers will react to a new product or to an improvement of an old one, executive judgment is put to a great test. This is because the techniques used in determining consumer attitudes and in measuring consumer behavior in relation to the product are very complex. Some of the consumer reaction measuring methods are totally foreign to the business world.

> Product quality is the number one side in a profitable marketing program, the package is the number two side, advertising is the number three side and pricing is number four. Actually, a marketing program depends on all four, equally. Weakness of any of the four sides will cut sales and diminish profits.

> Often the "image" symbolizes the company as a whole and serves as the focal point of the entire company

image. It performs as the hub of the company identity to the consumer and is a trademark that may have favorable or unfavorable connotations.

Several car designs should be parts of all tests merely as controls, as testing devices, not to be considered for actual production. This aspect is very important because it serves both as a control in the test situation, and as a means of keeping competition off the track. By conducting market tests on an unconscious level, by testing parts before finally testing complete car designs, and by including in these tests some designs as controls, we can get the answers for a car maker without revealing plans to competition.

The Sputniks made us more serious, more practical but not more rational. In 1958 I have seen more signs of psychological than of economic depression. The behavior of many still indicates a certain amount of desperation. The urging by some that we adopt communist methods in order to compete with Russia is irrational. The emphasis on physical science and willingness to neglect the humanities and the behavioral sciences in education is irrational. This irrational behavior, of course, was not predictable.

In order to find out what kind of label or package will motivate dog owners to buy a particular brand, we must conduct tests with controls. We must make sure that some factor outside of what is being tested, does not influence the respondents.

We can now hope to have non-irritating commercials on T.V., the kind that will be acceptable to theatre operators. We can anticipate such development in the advertising field because unconscious-level tests can be conducted to ascertain whether the public will react favorably toward the commercial and whether it will be effective in producing sales.

All of these research organizations, the pioneers and the imitators, have one thing in common. They all operate on the assumption that advertising is effective only on a conscious level, and that marketing is based on product familiarity. The great progress that has been made in the behavioral sciences in recent years is given no recognition. The findings of psychoanalysis are given no attention. The unconscious mind is given no consideration. Subconscious motivations are not measured.

The moment an individual is asked to judge and reveal his judgment, his defense mechanisms are immediately called into action. Ego-involvement and prestige identification immediately enter the test situation. Guards that operate both on conscious and unconscious levels take over the duties of protecting the ego and maintaining its privacy.

A physicist cannot predict the behavior of a single electron because the means he uses for observing or measuring its behavior changes its course. Therefore, he has to deal with great numbers of electrons in order to define their behavior. Human beings behave like electrons. A market researcher cannot predict the behavior of a single consumer because the means the researcher uses for observing or measuring the behavior often changes it. A market researcher has to deal with a great number of potential consumers in order to predict their pattern of behavior.

The management of Quality Bakers of America
Cooperative, Inc. became interested in motivation
research about ten years before the publication of this
book. Robert Schaus, Advertising Manager of QBA,
merchandisers of Sunbeam bread and other bakery
products, presented a marketing problem to Color
Research Institute in 1949.

The present symbol (oval with torch) of the Standard
Oil Company of Indiana was developed by creative
people with the aid of objective research under the
direction of Wesley Nunn almost fifteen years ago,
when scientific marketing was at the pioneering stage.

The following are articles in which automobile trends
were predicted more than a year before the publication
of this book!

INTRODUCTION

CHESKIN is a remarkable person. I have never known him to be wrong. One time when I said this to him, he replied that he was usually wrong but his research was right. I think this a good measure of the man—and of the book. He has been able to divorce his own personal likes, biases and personality from the research he does. He has been searching for "truth" independent of himself—or current fashions and fads in the research business.

By such a course of action he has run the risk of being labeled a maverick. However, his sole criterion of success is ability to predict success. And he is successful.

Probably no other person in this country could have developed the valid techniques that Cheskin has. The one main reason is the path that he took to market research. It is conceivable that an educator might become a top researcher but it is almost inconceivable that an artist would. But he owes a lot to art because it was his search for valid measurements of impact of colors and designs that led him to his techniques for testing on the "unconscious level."

When you work with colors, you work on the subsymbol level. There is a hierarchy of communication. At the top are words—high order symbols. Next there are illustrations and overt symbols such as crowns, crosses, etc. Then there is the sub-symbol world of color. Color is so primitive that color reactions may be closer to physiology than perception. Black and dark blue are perceived as the same color yet because blue is received by the color cones in the retina (and black is received by the rods) we experience a much fuller "perception" of black. This is the area in which Cheskin started. He discovered and refined his techniques at this sub-symbolic level and then carried them into the symbol area of package testing. Here the visual perceptions of form and color are most important, and also there is the opportunity to test the validity of testing methods.

Packaging offers an advertiser a wonderful vehicle for testing. The goods move off the shelf—or they don't. Also, there can be many experimental controls. Thus, Cheskin established techniques in color and design testing and proved the validity of them in the packaging field.

Now he has gone beyond packaging alone into the testing of print and electronic advertising. His techniques have gone through a development—but only after being proved on lower, more elemental levels. Most of us are forced to start at the highest testing level (advertising) where there are few sign posts to success. This is like trying to build a pyramid by starting with the top block.

The reader of this book may be looking for guidance in creative advertising—large picture, product shown in use, reader benefit, etc. He will not find it here. But he will find something more useable. The person who scans this book will get little. The person who reads this book will gain a philosophy about advertising. The person who studies this book will come away with a greater understanding of the forces which dominate and influence his own life.

Because of Cheskin's insistence upon objectivity he has contributed much to making marketing research a science and, as he points out, modern marketing research is as much a science as modern physics. In this book, he does not merely say so. He demonstrates and explains.

Are Cheskin's methods psychoanalytical or sociological? Is his research statistical or in depth? These questions simply do not apply. His research is not limited to any one school or type. It is all of the known kinds of research and more. He has no dogma. He merely is a problem solver. Because of this, his techniques and procedures have only one factor in common—ability to solve problems.

As the preface of this book shows, Cheskin is basically an educator. In the first two chapters, he approaches research from the management point of view. In the chapter "Dogs, Buyers and Sellers" he combines research with humor. In "Auto Makers' Problems Can Be Solved," he plays the role of critic of an industry.

In the chapter "Advertising of the Future," he gives many helpful suggestions for the advertising profession. In "How Scientific Can Research Be?" he draws parallels between marketing research and sub-atomic research. In "Why Is Research So Vital in Planning a New Product" he is Freudian and in other chapters he shows a statistical orientation.

Those readers interested in the eye-movement camera will learn that Cheskin has been using it for measuring eye-flow of marketing tools for fifteen years, and before that for non-commercial purposes. The use of the visibility camera for measuring one aspect of display effectiveness is also explained.

Today, the semantic differential is a current fad in advertising. However, fifteen years ago Cheskin began using what is now called semantic differential for measuring the effects of packages and ads. And he used it in connection with adult education almost a quarter of a century ago.

In *How to Predict What People Buy*, Cheskin reported about his pioneering work in marketing research. In *Why People Buy*, he reveals actual studies and discusses the principles in detail.

Each chapter in this book is instructive and revealing. One chapter, "How Scientific Can Marketing Research Be?", is the ultimate scientific answer to management men who are not using marketing research because they believe it is not scientific.

In the chapter "What Is and What Is Not Predictable," Cheskin reports on two studies, one in which a readership study based on interviews is compared with eye-movement tests, and a media study in which respondents tell in which medium they have seen certain products advertised. These two studies themselves make this book a good contribution to the marketing research field.

The book is filled with marketing research disclosures that are vital to every person in the marketing field. Brand managers and advertising men will profit greatly from reading *Why People Buy*. It has special significance to those in top management who are interested in or concerned with advertising and marketing consumer products.

HOWARD D. HADLEY

PREFACE

THOUGHTS of what was happening in my life twenty years ago come to my mind as I write this preface. In the fall of 1938, I completed the manuscript for my first book, *Living with Art*. It was published in 1940. I have just reviewed a number of the chapters in the book and they brought to my mind the idealism that motivated me. I have been told that idealism is quite evident to anyone who reads it.

To put down the "social-aesthetic" principles in the simplest possible language so that they would reach the greatest number of readers was quite a struggle. I remember the torturous job of cutting my original 425-page manuscript down to 200 pages. I was completely wrapped up in and dedicated the book to Adult Education.

Adult Education leaders liked the book. It is one of the most widely quoted and least read books. Authors refer to it, speakers quote from it, but few besides these have read it.

As a student and later a teacher, I could not understand how a modern, up-to-date Frenchman, like Matisse or Picasso, who enjoys all the fruits of an industrial society, becomes a primitive when he takes a hunk of clay or brush into his hand.

It could not be that the pillars of modern art, the giants of contemporary aesthetic expression suffered from schizophrenia. There was evidence that both Matisse and Picasso and the other kingpins of modern art were well adjusted to contemporary modes of living, in fact, to the luxuries of "streamlined" surroundings.

I was still more perplexed by the reactions of "art lovers" to various types of art. I heard a woman, who was educated in a finishing school and conditioned to either classical or Victorian art, exclaim, "How beautiful!", "What great feeling!", "Such wonderful originality!", as she gazed at a Picasso painting. I witnessed another heaping great praise on a Kandinsky abstract, but when I visited her home, I found it filled with French Provincial furniture. These two examples are typical of thousands of our contemporaries.

Finding out what made the "modem" artists do the things they do and what caused "art lovers" to behave as they do, became my primary goal.

To get the answers required probing the depths of human motivations. This is why I became interested in people's attitudes and became a researcher.

In 1935, the Adult Education Program of the Chicago Board of Education gave me the opportunity to fulfill my dream to put art to scientific measurement. Under the auspices of the Adult Education Program, I organized an Art Education Division, and set up a project for conducting studies on the psychological effects of visual media—designs, images and colors. Later a special project was organized for conducting studies on how visual media can be used as aids in motivating people to get interested in adult education. A special unit was formed for developing measuring instruments, testing devices, methods and techniques for evaluating attitudes.

For a short time, I directed a program in connection with the Federal Art Project, for training creative men and women in the graphic arts to communicate. Most of the creative people despised and resisted this program. To communicate meant to them limiting creativity and stifling originality. The program lasted about one year. The projects of the Board of Education were in operation from three to five years.

We were trying to measure attitudes toward adult education, toward citizenship, social studies, traditional and modern art.

A number of studies revealed the attitudes toward "adult education." They showed that the majority of men and women thought education was meant for the young, not for adults.

I decided to find out whether my book, *Living with Art*, did not become a best seller because it was not adequately promoted or for other reasons. A choice of one from five books was offered as a prize. This was only one part of the test, but the results of this part were quite revealing. Two of the books were novels, two were on modern art and the fifth was *Living with Art*. Test results: those respondents with art interests wanted one of the two on modern art. Respondents who had no art interests, about 80% of the sample, wanted one of the novels. *Living with Art* came out with a preference of 6%. It was quite clear that a very large majority of men and women were not interested in *Living with Art*.

This happened in 1940. I was busy directing a number of projects—with test forms, teaching plans and community programs; but "mercenary" ideas—had suddenly crept into my mind. What did this mean? I was toying with the idea of offering my services to commerce. I felt very guilty about this. I had been trained to be a teacher and researcher and had been conditioned to serve the general good, not do anything merely for a profit. Even my creative efforts in painting were to communicate, to inform, and seeking payment was supposed to be incidental or a necessary evil.

I was conscious of the fact that the Adult Education Program opened great vistas to me. I felt greatly obligated to the individuals who made it possible for me to have the experimental projects that gave me opportunities few persons have in a lifetime. I have always felt obligated to the late Elizabeth Wells Robertson and to Vernon Bowyer of the Chicago Board of Education, and I appreciated the aid I received from Harry T. Fultz and the late Clem O. Thompson of the University of Chicago. I felt close to the Adult Education movement and to the men and women who led it. It was difficult for me to break away.

However, "Pearl Harbor" accomplished for me what I couldn't do for myself. I was called to help save the world from Tojo and Hitler. While trying to teach soldiers how to recognize aircraft, how to camouflage themselves and how to do a job, no matter what it might be, in the shortest time and in the most efficient way, I had plenty of time to think. Although my thoughts were often interrupted, because I had an "errand to do" for the Colonel, I still found time for meditation.

During the war I met business people. In talking to them, I found out, much to my surprise, that they were investing millions on the basis of hunches. They discussed consumer products in rational terms. One told me that if you make the best mousetrap, the people will come to your door.

Very few had heard of the unconscious mind and of unconscious motivations. Most of those I talked with, some executives of large corporations, could not believe that a package, trademark or color could mean the difference between success and failure. By the time the war was almost over, I was convinced that I could make a major contribution to business.

However, I knew nothing about running a business. Like the character in search of an author, I was in search of a businessman who would run the business while I administered the services. I told a friend of mine, who was in the insurance business, that I needed a partner to whom business was not a mystery as it was to me. A few days later he invited me to his home for dinner where I met a man who was well known both as a business executive and as a public relations man. His name was George D. Gaw.

I showed George Gaw several examples of the research of images and colors from the experimental projects at the Board of Education. He examined them carefully and I was very flattered by his complimentary remarks.

He was particularly impressed with the studies on color.

"Businessmen and advertising men think they know a lot about design and copy, but they are aware that they know nothing about color," he said. This, I could understand.

He also told me about some "tests" he had done with color. They were extremely naive, with no controls whatever. But it was quite clear that George Gaw had a passion for color. He was running a service organization called "The Direct Mail Research Institute." He showed me a few of his releases. I saw that they contained many references to color. Most of them were reprints on color from popular magazines.

I saw the Direct Mail "literature" at his office at our second meeting. Our third was at the Chicago Board of Education offices where he asked me to come to his office on the following day to talk business.

The Direct Mail Research Institute was operating from the headquarters of the National Research Bureau. Gaw told me that the National Research Bureau would sell any services that had to do with research. This sounded good.

In less than a month I was installed as Associate Director of the Color Research Institute. This was in September of 1944. We thought the war was almost over, but after a number of weeks of Color Research Institute activity, the Allied troops had a setback in Holland and affairs in general looked bleak to me.

Soon, world affairs began to improve and we continued to organize the Color Research Institute. George Gaw introduced me to Bill Wood, President of the National Research Bureau, who confirmed what Gaw had told me. The National Research Bureau would sell the Color Research Institute services. Gaw brought in a man who had been in the billboard advertising business and the wife of Gaw's nephew who had for some time been in the direct mail business with him. She took charge of the secretarial work.

In the early part of 1945, we received our state charter. We were the Color Research Institute of America, George D. Gaw, President and Director; Louis Cheskin, Executive Vice President and Associate Director. Bill Wood served as Director of Sales until May, 1947, when we moved to new quarters.

We were set to conduct studies in marketing effectiveness of all media. Although we all used the words research, color, design and copy, it soon became obvious to me that we did not mean the same things. The objective was for National Research Bureau to get something from Color Research Institute to sell, and my ideas were not saleable.

I had no idea what selling was all about. And I was a minority of one.

It became quite clear that what color meant to me, the information that I had accumulated on color in my experimental work in connection with the Adult Education Program, should be put into a book. I was convinced that I had to go on record. I had to set down what was already known, so that necessary experiments could be made clear and there would be no confusion about what is known and unknown in the field of color and design.

I began to work feverishly on *Colors: What They Can Do for You*, which was published in 1947. Color as it applies to almost every phase of life is treated in this book. One chapter deals with color in marketing, another with color in industry and still another with color in art. Fashions are covered. The physical, chemical, physiological and psychological aspects of color are discussed in direct, everyday, simple language. Basically, I was still in adult education.

Several titles for the book had been tested. *Colors: What They Can Do for You* received the greatest acceptance, and it became the title of the book. In 1948, there was a new printing. The book was a success.

It soon became evident that George Gaw was right in at least one respect. Communication about color was very poor. We had been using the Ostwald system, the best available, at that time produced by Container Corporation, as a means of communication. We designated colors for our clients by an Ostwald notation.

However, we were continually getting into hot water. The Ostwald system charts did not contain enough colors. There were fewer than one thousand color chips. The chips were in dye, on acetate, and we were designating most of the colors to be used in printing ink on paper. Matching was very difficult. Still a third limitation was that the Ostwald charts provided no guidance for reproducing the colors. I had to get busy to devise a more adequate system for color designation, communication and guidance.

After almost two years of experimenting, I developed a system containing 4800 colors derived from the three, subtractive or substance primaries (process colors) used by printers. I split the three primaries into forty-eight equidistant hues. (I tried a greater split and found that identity was completely lost in the blue-red range.) Then I diluted each hue with additions of white in nine equidistant steps downward. (This was accomplished by using Ben Day screens.) Then I prepared a black plate consisting of nine tonal values, running from lightest (10%) at the extreme left and deepest (90%) at the extreme right. By superimposing the black plate upon the color plate, the result was that each chart had 100 equidistant colors. Since each of the forty-eight hues was treated the same way, there were 4800 colors. This color system, known as the CHESKIN COLOR CHARTS, was published in 1949.

Although I was writing articles and giving interviews for business publications, clients told me that there should be a book specially for businessmen. Many of them felt that *Colors: What They Can Do for You* covered too wide a field, that it was more like an encyclopedia on color. There should be a book on color and design based on Color Research Institute studies to meet the particular needs of marketing people.

Because of the urging from many, I took the chapter on merchandising from *Colors: What They Can Do for You* and expanded it into a book. I used the same simple, direct style in presenting the basic facts about color and design in marketing.

A number of titles were tested with potential readers of the book and *Color for Profit* came out most favorably in the tests. It was published in 1951.

Color for Profit did not contain color charts. The CHESKIN COLOR CHARTS with 4800 equidistant colors were found to be too large and too expensive for the average person.

Therefore, I designed a set of junior color charts. I developed a system for producing 300 colors by running the charts through the press four times, with process inks. There are 12 charts in the set with 25 colors on each. The three printing primaries are made into 12 hues and each hue is converted to 25 colors by equidistant steps of white and/or black. These charts were produced in 1952 with printing codes, showing the primary color content of each color on the charts.

I was told by a representative of a book publishing company that there was a great demand for color wheels, that the available ones were inadequate. They showed hues and tints, but no shades and tones. In 1953, I produced a color wheel with 360 colors—12 hues, 348 tints, shades and tones. On the CHESKIN COLOR WHEEL, tones and shades are produced by rotating a transparent disk with five tonal value screens.

Our field testing division was expanding rapidly and we needed devices for getting the cooperation of respondents in testing marketing tools—packages, ads, etc. Primarily for the purpose of motivating respondents, I wrote a booklet called *Color Tuning Your Home*. This booklet was used very successfully in getting housewives interested in Color Research Institute marketing tests.

The booklet was shown to a chief editor of a book publishing company, and he asked me to expand it into a full book. *How to Color-Tune Your Home* was published in 1954. The title was changed from *Color Tuning Your Home* to *How to Color-Tune Your Home* on the basis of a test with potential readers of the book.

Before the publication of *How to Color-Tune Your Home*, I received more criticism from clients. Many of them found *Color for Profit* too limited in scope. It dealt with basic psychological principles and basic design and color principles. It did not deal with the entire problem of producing a printed marketing tool. It did not show how various professions are involved and did not indicate a coordinated effort of many individuals. "There should be a book that traces the complete process of creating an ad or a package from the idea to the printed page," said a client to me.

This seemed like a practical idea. I asked the publishing company of *How to Color-Tune Your Home* whether they would publish such a book, and they expressed interest. I wrote the book in less than six months, because most of the material was in Color Research Institute files. A number of titles were tested with businessmen and advertising executives. *Color Guide for Marketing Media* came out best in the tests. It was published in 1954, the same year as *How to Color-Tune Your Home.* The latter was published in early spring, the former in the fall. The Junior Color Charts with 300 colors are parts of both books. However, the printing codes are only in *Color Guide for Marketing Media.*

Of course, none of the so-called color books deal only with color. There is no such thing as abstract color. Color is part of form and space. Thus, *Color for Profit* and *Color Guide for Marketing Media* actually deal with practical problems in the graphic media. Imagery, design, pattern are covered. The creative aspects, the psychological factors and the measurement of marketing effectiveness are discussed.

How to Color-Tune Your Home includes the psychological aspects of color and furniture, of form and arrangement. The nature of color and its application to practical problems in the home are discussed. Actual experiments with colors are reported. Designs and arrangements of home furnishings are covered.

By 1950, there were many things happening besides the demand for books. I became convinced that salesmanship and research are like oil and water—they don't mix. A friend said I had become obsessed with the idea that research, like medicine, should be offered, made available, not sold.

Perhaps he was right that I was obsessed with the idea. I knew I had to be free to tell a client that he did not need a field test, if I knew that we had the information in our files. I had to feel free to tell him that ocular measurements were all his problem needed, that field tests were not needed, if I knew this was so. All this meant that salesmen had no place in the Color Research Institute picture because a salesman's objective is to sell as much as possible for as big a fee as possible.

After almost six years of seeing research "sold," I separated research from salesmanship. In the fall of 1951, I organized everything on a purely service basis. I also eliminated all the technical color services that had to do with color printing. We went about quietly getting our share of marketing research from our regular clients and were kept busy getting out reports on ocular measurements, color and image ratings and field tests of brand images, packages and some ads.

By 1957, it became apparent that Color Research Institute was no longer the only organization or almost the only one in the field of motivation research. When my articles on "unconscious level testing" were published in business publications in 1947 and 1948, little attention was paid to them. But ten years later, marketing research people and marketing and advertising executives began to discover the validity of tests that are conducted with indirect methods. Many were emulating Color Research Institute.

In the spring of 1957, Vance Packard's *The Hidden Persuaders* was published and motivation researchers sprouted by the dozen. Motivation research was discussed in all business and advertising circles, and the marketing research profession became divided into two camps. In one camp were the traditional researchers who conduct polls, readership studies, impact measurements, recall tests and interviews with consumers on their preferences. In the other were the motivation researchers who employ unstructured projective techniques and depth interviews.

Since Color Research Institute conducts motivation research

with controlled techniques and because it employs traditional statistical forms, it remained outside of both camps.

Vance Packard classified me with Dichter and Gardner and with some who are not actually in the field of motivation research.

The Hidden Persuaders seemed to make almost everyone motivation research conscious and it aroused many people against motivation research. The implication in Packard's book is that motivation researchers are manipulators.

Actually, what Packard points out is, that some individuals misuse motivation research, that they could use it for anti-social purposes and that there are some who would, if they could, use motivation research against the interests of the people.

This is true about almost everything. Language can be used to say good and true things, and it can be used to make evil and false statements. Motivation research can be used for good or evil. It depends on who uses it and for what purpose.

It became quite clear that I had to take quick action to accomplish the following. One, produce evidence that motivation research is not new, as many seemed to think; that Color Research Institute had been in the business of motivation research for over a dozen years. Two, that there is nothing insidious or anti-social about motivation research; that it is merely a means for finding out what people really want. Because people cannot always tell us what they like or why they like an object or product, we use special techniques for getting this information.

After a number of conferences at the Color Research Institute offices, it was decided that the most important articles that have been published in the last ten years about the marketing media testing activities of Color Research Institute, written by me and by others, should be published in book form.

Since documentation was of primary importance, it was best, we thought, to use the articles in the original form. I was well aware that such a book would not be a piece of original literature.

In order to give unity to the book and to give it a natural

starting point, I wrote four new special articles and arranged to have them published in business publications. I asked Van Allen Bradley, editorial writer and book critic of the *Chicago Daily News*, to help us choose sixteen articles out of some forty that have appeared since 1947. Twenty articles, including the four new ones, were assembled into manuscript form. Bradley volunteered to write an introduction.

After testing a number of titles, *How to Predict What People Will Buy* was published in early fall of 1957.

Perhaps, largely due to its coming out when *The Hidden Persuaders* was still on the best seller list, *How to Predict What People Will Buy* became a success, considering the nature of the book. It was displayed in many bookstore windows with *The Hidden Persuaders*.

Many individuals in the marketing research field did not welcome its appearance in marketing literature, of course. However, it was reviewed favorably in most of the business press and was received with enthusiasm in most business circles. It is considered by many, and it was meant to be, a primer in motivation research. It is a documented record of the pioneering and progress in controlled motivation research methods and techniques. It is a key to a dozen years of testing marketing media on an unconscious level.

Most of the chapters were written by me. Some were originally interviews with me written by journalists.

Some of the chapters in *How to Predict What People Will Buy* are elementary in character. This fact attracts many readers and alienates some.

A number of criticisms came to me on *How to Predict What People Will Buy*. "You should write a book that goes deeper into motivation research," one friend said to me. Another thought that I should tell more about testing techniques. A third person expressed the opinion that I should reveal a little of how ads and filmed commercials are tested on an unconscious level. A fourth thought that I should address management and point out to management why it should use marketing research. A fifth suggested that I should tell about my background and how I began testing on an unconscious level.

It became clear that there was need for another book on controlled marketing research. In this book, I cover what was not covered in *How to Predict What People Will Buy*.

I named this book *Why People Buy*. It is a definitive book. It begins with "Basis for Management Decision" and ends with reports of actual studies. In the testing procedures, we do not ask consumers why they buy and they don't tell us. However, controlled tests, that I describe, reveal what motivates people to buy and what does not. In essence, this means the tests show why they buy. Either "What Motivates People to Buy" or "What Makes Them Buy," which represents literally what the book deals with, would be a clumsy and awkward title. Therefore, the book is called *Why People Buy*.

CHAPTER 1

BASIS FOR MANAGEMENT DECISION

I REMEMBER my father saying about a man who was a great financial success, that he was a "shrewd businessman." I heard him say on another occasion, that another friend of his was lucky in business; "everything he touches turns into gold." These two evaluations are typical of my father's and grandfather's generation. Even now there are executives, some in large corporations, who make marketing decisions on hunches or conjecture.

The "scientific" approach to marketing is still not used by many organizations. Many manufacturers, who have adopted scientific production methods and scientifically organized production management, still do not plan marketing programs on the basis of facts. Comparatively few executives of small businesses make marketing forecasts on the basis of scientifically controlled market research. The scientific approach to marketing is still new.

Many of the large corporations use various types of marketing research on which they rely and use as a basis for executive judgment. Most executives in large corporations use research on sales of competitive brands, test markets and some other types of check points in planning their marketing programs.

A well-planned marketing program has a specific goal and an operating budget. A marketing plan incorporates an estimate of future sales based on some specific measures of consumer acceptance and marketing conditions.

Economic conditions are not static. Often competitive action could not have been anticipated and given consideration in the initial plan. For either of these two reasons, sales results may not be in accordance with the goals or estimated sales performance. But in a complex market such as ours, management must have marketing plans with specific goals and budgets and operational controls with frequent and regular evaluations of sales results.

If marketing conditions are changed, either because of a general change in our economy or because of the action of competition, the predetermined plan has to be changed on the basis of the new conditions. Whether conditions have changed sufficiently to revise the original plan or whether a special effort should be made to reach the original goal to meet a marketing threat is in the realm of management judgment and decision.

Some executives, particularly heads of small businesses, take this position: "What's the use of making an elaborate marketing plan, if it has to be changed every three months?" The answer, of course, is that if you don't have a plan of operations, if you don't have an operating budget, you are not equipped to make quick changes in the marketing operation to meet the new conditions. You can compare the new marketing conditions with the old ones, if you have a map, a chart or a clear picture of the old conditions. You can have no accurate evaluation of new marketing conditions without having an evaluation of the market for which you originally prepared yourself.

Management can manage efficiently only if it has a clear picture of the interdependent operations of planning and checking, evaluation and control. Management has to provide the initiative and guidance for the planning. It has to evaluate the sales results in the light of the original plan and to control the adjustment to new marketing conditions.

Big business has to operate in this scientific manner. Small businesses have a much greater chance of success or of becoming bigger businesses by using scientific planning and operation. To meet the conditions of a highly competitive market, management has to use a scientific approach to the marketing problems, as well as to the manufacturing operations.

Management's function is qualitative in each area and in each role. A business will be most successful if the planning is based not merely on any marketing information, but on the most reliable kind of marketing facts. It is management that has to decide which of the available fact gathering methods or agencies have validity and are the most reliable.

There are many market research organizations whose main activities consist of auditing markets, geographic areas, size, character, income level and educational backgrounds of potential consumers. Not all organizations providing this type of information use the same methods of auditing. Some are more reliable than others. Management has to decide which of the available market auditing organizations will provide the best information for market planning.

In the field of predetermining how consumers will react to a new product or to an improvement of an old one, executive judgment is put to a great test. This is because the techniques used in determining consumer attitudes and measuring consumer behavior in relation to the product are very complex. Some of the consumer reaction measuring methods are totally foreign to the business world.

Research techniques for measuring what motivates shoppers were developed outside of the marketing field. Purchase behavior is psychological. Motivations of shoppers are not totally or even basically rational and, therefore, the normal, direct procedures for measuring objective factors are not valid.

Often, the rational aspects of a product have no appeal to consumers. The functional or practical character does not always motivate consumers to buy the product. Management must find devices that will appeal to the potential consumers or users of the product. Emotional appeals, not rational ones, have to be used. Management must find the kind of appeals that will motivate people to buy the product. For this, executives have to go outside of the traditional marketing area.

Special types of research have shown executives of insurance companies that they can sell much more insurance by selling "security in old age" and "security of family" instead of an insurance policy. Cosmetics manufacturers have learned from research, directly or indirectly, that they can increase their volume of sales greatly by selling "beauty," instead of cold cream, lipstick or face powder. A well known soap manufacturing company found that it had increased sales greatly by selling "purity," instead of just plain soap.

Emotional appeals did not originate in the production plant. The behavioral sciences are the source of such sales appeals. Because the behavioral sciences are new and are not in tune with traditional concepts, management has to be very careful in making decisions on which of the techniques or procedures are valid for solving a particular consumer appeal problem.

In a complex and highly competitive marketing situation as exists today, a mere announcement of a new product is not sufficient. Persuasion must be used. A great variety of appeals are devised by marketing and advertising specialists. Special methods and techniques have to be used for determining which of these appeals is the most effective in motivating people to buy the product. Executive judgment comes into play in making a choice of an agency, or techniques that are to be used, for measuring the relative effectiveness of several appeals to consumers.

Traditionally, entire marketing programs have been based on the personal judgment of the executive. Executive decision is still here. It is still the guiding hand of every marketing program. Now the decision is on which of the research techniques should be used, in order to have maximum scientific control in marketing as well as in production.

Consumers make decisions in the market place, sometimes consciously and frequently unconsciously. Consumers are generally not aware of what motivates them to buy one brand instead of another. However, executives have to make their decisions consciously when they are confronted with diverse avenues of action. The decisions of executives or managers have an effect on the behavior or actions of their subordinates. In other words, the decisions of executives have an effect not only on their own behavior, but also on the actions of others. Such decisions cannot be made unconsciously or subjectively in a functioning business.

In making a decision, the executive must be aware of action alternatives. He must evaluate them before he can make a decision. In evaluating the alternatives he may rely on his personal experience. He may depend on sketchy information that he had once received and which still lingers in his memory. He may consult his subordinates, each of whom also has a slight knowledge about the problem, or he may rely on information derived from thorough research of one or more kinds, from one or more sources. There is evidence that executives in successful business organizations generally make their marketing decisions on the basis of reliable research.

For most modem, up-to-date executives, market research provides support in each phase of market planning. One type of market research is designed for the purpose of evaluating the potential market and predicting the rate of development of the market. A second is used for predicting consumer attitudes toward a specific product design or product character. A third is employed to determine the best marketing theme or the most effective selling strategy. A fourth is used for measuring the production capacity of the organization. And research is also used for determining what will motivate personnel—sales personnel, production personnel, shipping personnel, office personnel, etc.

Qualitative research is used where it is necessary to learn about the kind of action or kind of product. Purely quantitative research is used to get a measure of how much action or how much of a product there should be in a given time or place.

The modern executive uses "scientific" methods as a guide in making decisions. Modern, up-to-date management is "scientific management." Modern, up-to-date executives practice "scientific marketing." This means that business decisions are made by managers on what is considered to be factual support.

"Scientific management," say some, is not as exact as "true" science. It is not based on absolute principles. However, this should not make us hesitate to use the term "scientific" in relation to business. Modern physicists do not consider physics absolute. Classical physics is as obsolete now as is nineteenth century industry. Einstein, Bohr, Planck, Heisenberg and others have discovered elements in nature that are not in the structure of Newton's physics. There are no absolutes in atomic physics.

I should at this point call attention to one kind of decision making practiced in many corporations which is not scientifically sound, yet is not based on the subjective opinion or limited knowledge of the manager or a subordinate. I have in mind the committee method of decision making. Sometimes this is called the democratic method. It is also known as the brain picking method or brain storming method. This often operates on the assumption that a number of uninformed people can arrive at a better decision than one uninformed person.

Decision making in a marketing program is frequently and crucially in the area of communication, in finding an effective means of persuading potential consumers to buy the particular product or brand.

Persuading means influencing opinions or affecting attitudes by means of communication. It means not only informing, but educating, plus motivating. It means affecting the hearts as well as the minds of people.

To persuade a person, the message has to reach his emotions, not merely his sense of logic. If the message contradicts an individual's opinions, beliefs or attitudes, the individual will reject the message or will have no interest in it.

Many advertising men fail to realize that a sales message delivered is not the same as a sales message received.

A communication about a product is one thing. But people paying attention to it, believing it and being motivated by it is another matter entirely.

An unconvincing message is either rejected outright or is modified to fit the opinion of the person who sees it or hears it. For a message to be effective it must fit a goal of the individual who receives the message, it must satisfy an emotional need. The message must motivate the individual.

There is no longer any question among serious students of psychology whether people are rational or irrational. We know that individuals are motivated by both emotional and rational factors. A message has to have emotional appeal and at the same time possess rational or practical elements.

A number of questions have to be answered in planning any kind of message on which many thousands of dollars will be spent. The questions are particularly hard to answer if the message is of the persuasion type. Is the message addressed in the most effective way? Is the timing the best? Does it appeal to the particular people it is supposed to reach? Is it easily recalled? Is it confused by people with another message from another source? Does it impress only those who agree with the message or does it have a favorable effect on people who ordinarily would not agree with it?

For a message to fail in persuading, it does not necessarily have to antagonize people. Indifference to the message means that the communication is weak.

Managers can, and some do, use research to get answers to these questions. Some research discloses the kind of people and how many are reached by the message. Other research shows how many are favorably affected by the communication, how many are unfavorably affected and how many indifferent to it.

However, research can play its role only after there is something to test. First, creative individuals have to compose the message.

Generally, a number of approaches are used; several themes are tried. The message is composed in many forms. Executives have to decide which of these forms, in which of the several ways, the communication will be most effective.

Executives use some basic principles in nuking such decisions. One device used by advertising executives is the "principle of association," which is demonstrated in the use of a pretty girl for selling a soft drink, or a rugged individual for selling cigarettes. It is known that most people, men and women, like to look at pretty girls. If a bottle of the particular brand of beverage is shown next to the girl, those who look at the girl will automatically see the brand of beverage. The "principle of association" becomes still stronger when the message communicates the idea that this pretty girl drinks this particular beverage.

The "association principle" operates in the same way in selling cigarettes by associating the brand of cigarettes with an appealing, rugged, he-man character. This interesting man not only attracts people to the cigarettes, but the message communicates that men such as he, smoke this brand of cigarettes.

The "association principle" is understood by advertising and public relations men and women. However, executives of the communications media still have questions that they cannot answer. They do not know what type of girl will appeal to the greatest number of people or what type will appeal to the particular individuals for whom the message is intended. They do not know exactly what kind of a man will have greatest appeal to the largest group. If the executives decide to use a rugged character as the symbol, they must delineate this character. They need a specific image of the character.

This is where research is again called upon. Creative individuals produce images, photographs, paintings and drawings of sportsmen, cowboys, sailors and other rugged types. Research is called upon to measure the relative effectiveness of these images.

Before management is ready to consider the character of the

advertising or the nature of the communication about the product, it has to make sure that the product itself presents a favorable image. Here too, the "principle of association" is used. Orange juice is served with Castor oil to children by mothers in order to make the Castor oil acceptable. The same principle is used in marketing. An instrument that may suggest danger to people is encased in streamlined form and pleasing color. The image of smooth form and appealing color overshadows the image of danger that people might have.

Here too, management has to get answers to a number of questions. What kind of form or styling will have the most favorable effect on the greatest number of potential buyers of the product? What color will have the most favorable effect and motivate the greatest number of people to want the product? The right kind of research can provide the answers to these questions.

The present-day executive must be a problem-solver. He has to approach each problem without getting emotionally involved. He must make decisions on the basis of objective information.

An executive can find solutions to problems. He can find new ways for solving new problems if he is aware that naturally or emotionally he is likely to be indifferent to or even hostile to a new idea, that is, to a concept that is not within the realm of his experience. If he recognizes this, he will guard himself against it.

The modern executive is aware that new ideas are not necessarily good ideas. He uses modern research for determining whether the idea is good or bad. Modern research is "scientific research." Scientific means controlled.

A physicist cannot tell in what manner or how far a ball will roll on the street. He can determine how a specific ball will behave in a specific place, under specific circumstances or conditions. The physicist can obtain the answers to an unknown if all the other factors are known. In other words, he must test the unknown under controlled conditions.

Managers of consumer goods manufacturing companies are

generally consumer oriented. When planning to introduce a new product, the executives give primary attention to the potential consumers. Some executives want research that will show people's wants, that is, whether they want such a product or a particular form of the product. Others want to know whether people will accept the product, although they do not care about why they accept it. Still others are interested in finding out not only what people will accept or what they want, but also why they accept it or want it.

Some marketing executives operate on the assumption that people do not know what they want. To these executives, marketing means creating wants, that is, making people want what they have to sell. Before air conditioners were introduced to the market, people did not want air conditioners. The wants were created by making air conditioners available and by demonstrating the advantages of air conditioners.

However, people did want to be cool on hot days. The first question to be answered was not whether people wanted air conditioners, but whether they wanted to be cool in the hot weather season. The want to be cool existed. In a competitive market the marketer had to create a want for his particular brand or for his special way of keeping cool.

From a purely rational point of view, most people don't always want what they need and they don't always need what they want. For example, a woman may need a fur coat to keep warm so she won't catch cold in near zero weather, but she wants a mink stole. She knows the mink stole will not keep her warm, but she wants it for other reasons, psychological reasons which are motivating.

There are biological needs and social needs; practical needs and psychological needs. All the various needs are basic wants. The marketer does not create the wants, he merely satisfies them. The marketer generally has to convince people that his product or brand satisfies their wants.

People are not always conscious of their wants. Because they are not always aware of what they actually want, they cannot tell you. Special techniques and procedures have to be used to get people to reveal their wants without their realizing that they are expressing their desires. They may have guilt feelings about their wishes.

Basically, human wants are all about the same. We all want comfort, love and happiness. Individual wants are conditioned by environmental and social factors.

There are still many executives who assume that all human beings have exactly the same wants. There are many managers who operate on the assumption that if the products are good for them, they are good for others. "I like the product, I want it," he says to himself, "therefore, most people will want it." Such an executive is not aware that his social position, his financial status, his education, perhaps his background make his reactions to an object totally different from the reactions of an average person. Such an executive is, of course, not in the class of "scientific management."

The executives who are in the class of "scientific management" make judgments on the basis of objective information only. I have already outlined the various types of research that are used for gathering specific types of information.

Some of the necessary information is of a purely quantitative nature. Research techniques for gathering such information are well established. Marketing problems in which people's attitudes are involved and in which motivating factors have to be evaluated are not in the realm of quantitative research techniques.

Attitudes, multiple motivations, conflicting wishes and unconscious reactions are not in the sphere of mere head counting. Psychological needs, cultural influences, and social pressures cannot be verbalized by consumers.

Research that records what people say does not reveal their true wants. Only the type of research that discloses natural, uninhibited reactions, real feelings, true attitudes and preferences in which self-interest is involved can be considered valid. This type of research did not develop in the climate of the business world but in the area of the behavioral sciences.

The basic principles and research techniques were borrowed from the field of psychology, particularly from psychoanalysis and from Gestalt psychology. The techniques have been modified and adapted to marketing needs. These techniques are now highly developed. They have been used successfully for solving marketing problems for about fifteen years. They provide a basis for management decision.

CHAPTER 2

THE STRUCTURE OF A MARKETING PROGRAM

IN A CASUAL conversation at an informal gathering, a man said he was having some trouble with his digestion and was going to see a doctor. One of the group suggested that he see a specialist in this particular ailment. "Oh no," my friend said, "I don't like specialists. They cure their specialty instead of your actual trouble." This statement made me think that marketing, like medicine, is full of specialists, each seeing his specialty as the only or most important element in a marketing situation.

Advertising people generally operate on the premise that the advertising theme or plan, plus a big budget, is the key to any marketing success. The introduction of the Edsel is an excellent example of maximum concentration on advertising and promotion.

Obviously, the 1958 Edsel was launched on the assumption that the design of the car was not a vital factor in marketing an automobile and that the name of the car was of minor importance. The name could be chosen for sentimental reasons, those in charge must have reasoned, since, after all, the advertising and promotion will be the biggest and best ever.

The marketing failure of the 1958 Edsel is one demonstration of the falsity of the assumption that with a big advertising budget and great promotion campaign you can sell anything.

Another demonstration that a big advertising budget is not all that is needed to sell a product is the case of a manufacturer of a breakfast food. The agency for the breakfast food was interested in developing a new marketing theme. The agency men decided that in order to get a fresh sales approach, they needed a new package. They sold management on the idea and a new package design was created.

When the marketing effectiveness of the new package design was measured by means of tests conducted on an unconscious level, it failed to pass the tests. The brand managers and the agency executives did not like the test results which contradicted their opinions and were not in tune with the marketing theme they conceived.

The research findings were disregarded and the new packages were produced and delivered to the stores. However, they remained on the store shelves. Although a big advertising campaign backed the introduction of the new package, the old consumers did not recognize the brand in the new packages and the new packages did not attract new consumers.

The company was forced to discontinue the new packages and cut off the new campaign. The old familiar package reappeared on the market.

The launching of the 1958 Edsel car and the introduction of a new package for an old brand of breakfast food are both excellent examples demonstrating that an advertising campaign by itself, no matter how good or how big, does not assure having a successful marketing program.

Not only advertising specialists are often guilty of considering their special field the only major factor in marketing. Package designers frequently stress packaging above everything else.

Designers are creative individuals. They love to create new ideas and new forms. They naturally strive to change. They normally consider everything that is new superior to everything that is old.

The greatest contribution of designers is their originality and creativity, which can, under some conditions, be negative factors in marketing.

Consumers in general are tired of the old, but fear the new. They are stimulated by and are also made to feel insecure by the new. Many people are attracted by new objects and new forms, but they resist them because they are strange. Although the old forms and objects give people feelings of security, they are often boring or unstimulating.

Research has shown that people readily accept something new about the old. The old part makes them feel secure and confident; the new aspect is stimulating and interesting.

The question is how much of the old and how much new should there be in a product in order for it to have maximum consumer acceptance?

We get the answer to questions of this kind from research, the kind of research that reveals true consumer attitudes and shows actual behavior of consumers in relation to the product or article.

Such research has disclosed that a new package is not always more effective than the old one, that the package of good taste is not always the best marketing tool and that the most original design is not always the best for a particular product. Marketing experience has later confirmed the results of tests that were conducted on an unconscious level.

Sales people often have their eyes focused at one point. They are frequently guilty of considering aggressive selling techniques as the most important factors in marketing. Sales managers are apt to disregard everything else in a marketing program and stress only aggressive selling. They put all emphasis on the sales pitch and on beating the pavements.

Sales specialists often stress competitive pricing as the key to increasing the volume of sales. If the product does not move fast enough, lower the price, is the dictum of many a sales manager.

Too rare is the sales manager who studies the nature of the advertising or looks into the effectiveness of the package or point of sale material.

Production men also are generally over-specialized. They, too, are immersed in production problems and often fail to see the company-and-consumer relationship as a whole or the marketing side.

The automotive engineer is convinced that the car having the best engine will have the greatest sale. The average engineer can't understand or believe that styling has more to do with selling a car than the engine. It makes no sense to him.

The production manager of a candy manufacturing plant could not believe that the candy with the most expensive ingredients did not have the greatest consumer acceptance. Quality is an objective reality to a production man. Good is good for everybody. The best is the best for all, according to many production managers.

Our highly industrialized, complex society must have specialists. Knowledge has become so wide and great that no one person can possibly know all or even the basic principles of more than one or two fields of knowledge. We must rely on specialists. However, we should always keep in mind the weaknesses or dangers inherent in specialization.

Specialists generally look for their specialty. They are apt to overlook the real weakness, the true source of trouble, because they look with the eyes of the specialist. They find only what they look for because they unconsciously and naturally look for the thing in which they specialize.

When I was a boy I heard the following story: A benevolent ruler of a city state was reaching the age of retirement. He was making plans to hand over the governing duties to one of his assistants. He could not decide which of two would be the better ruler. Both of them flattered him and catered to his wishes. But what would either one of them do if he were master? That was the question. So the wise old man sent the two young men out to do a research job. Each was given an assignment to make a journey to a well known distant city state to study its people. He wanted a report on the integrity, honesty, diligence and cooperative spirit of the residents of that city state.

One young man brought back a report that this city state was full of rascals, gangsters, crooks and ne'er-do-wells.

The other young man's report disclosed that the citizens of that city state were good, honest, hard-working and cooperative.

Each of them found the kind of people he was looking for. The one who looked for goodness found it. The other who searched for evil found it.

All of us are apt to see things according to our own yardsticks. We generally find what we are looking for, and too often we fail to see anything that we are not looking for, no matter how vital it may be.

To assure success, marketing men must guard against this danger. They must look at all the four sides of the marketing structure. They must examine all four walls that support the marketing roof. They must concentrate on all the sides that make profit possible.

The Product

The most important side of the marketing structure is the product. A product that is not as good as that of competition is not likely to be a great success, no matter how good everything else is.

A strong promotion, a large advertising budget or an appealing package may make the first sale to the consumer. But for repeat sales, the product must be at least as good as that of competition.

Better still, is having a product that is superior to that of competition. A superior product means superior in the eyes of consumers. It does not necessarily mean superior in terms of objective values or according to laboratory standards. The following examples show that actual value or cost and consumers' concepts of value are not always the same.

In a test with consumers of four kinds of candy, we found that the most costly candy did not have great consumer acceptance.

Four types of imported silk yard goods were tested with consumers. The finest silk had low preference, about as low as the poorest quality. The second best, or the second highest in cost, had the highest consumer preference, regardless of price.

Neckties ranging from $1.00 to $10.00 in value were offered as prizes. Each person was free to take any tie he wanted. The $5.00 ties had the greatest acceptance, the $7.50 ties were second highest in preference and the $2.50 ties were a close third. The $10.00 ties and the $1.00 ties were taken by very few.

Six makes of suits were offered as prizes to men who participated in a test. The values of the suits were $45, $75, $95, $125, $175 and $225. The greatest number of choices were for the $125 suit. The $175 suit was a close second and the $95 one was third. The $75 suit and the $225 one had few takers. The $45 suit had no takers.

These are a few of many examples illustrating that actual quality is not the same as consumer acceptance or the consumer's idea of quality. This is true in all fields and with all products.

Because objective standards are not always the same as consumers' standards, a new product should be tested with consumers before it is put on the market. It should be made up in various experimental forms and reliable research people should be employed to test its acceptance with consumers.

After you have ascertained that you have a product that meets consumers' concepts of quality, you have to investigate the second side of the marketing structure, the package.

The Package

For the present-day market, a product has to be packaged or styled or both. A food, a drug or a cosmetic needs a container. A machine has to be endowed with pleasing form and attractive color.

Generally, people know little about the actual product. They habitually judge a book by its cover, a grocery product by its label, a drugstore product by its bottle and an automobile by the styling.

Packaging is the second most important side or wall of a marketing structure. The package is second in importance only to the product itself. It represents the product. The package is a visual image of the product. It is the symbol. The consumer does not judge the product, he judges the package. The package tells the shopper whether the product is of high or low quality, whether it is the kind of a product he wants or does not want.

A quarter of a century ago, the package was merely a physical container. It was a measuring and handling device. It was designed to protect the product. Under present marketing conditions, the package is a psychological factor. It is a marketing tool. It is a silent salesman.

The package is no longer merely physical in character. It is no longer simple. In fact, the common, typical, present-day package is very complex. It has a brand-identifying image. It has a brand name. It has form and pattern or design. It has color. It has components such as instructions or recipes, premium offers and product illustrations, usually in the final, usable form. Any package that has these elements, not of the best, is not an effective marketing tool.

The brand name can be the key to success or failure of a marketing program. A half a century ago, a car with the unpronounceable (at that time) name, Chevrolet, could become a success because any carriage that could move without a horse pulling it was automatically a success.

Nowadays, there are many cars of equal quality in performance, fighting for the consumer's dollar. A brand name, therefore, is of great importance. A name is a symbol. It may symbolize high quality or low quality. It may be a symbol of reliability or lack of it. It may be favorably associated with the product or unfavorably. It may motivate people to buy the product or a competitive product of equal quality or performance.

Compare Thunderbird with Edsel. Both cars are made by Ford. The Thunderbird suggests action. It has appropriate symbolism. What does Edsel symbolize? It is the name of a gentleman. It is the name of the man who was the head of the company that manufactures the car. What kind of an image does it bring to your mind? What symbolism does it have? What association does it have with the character of the particular car? What does it mean? The name is no doubt one of the major reasons why the new 1958 Edsel was not a marketing success.

Research shows that the brand-identifying image is a vital part of every effective package. It is the focal point. It is a brand-identifying device. It has symbolic meaning. It has quality or lack of quality connotations.

A package without a brand-identifying image that is appealing to consumers and easily remembered is very rarely an effective marketing tool. Excellent examples of brands with effective brand-identifying images are the following: Standard Oil of Indiana, Good Luck margarine, Dove, Parliament cigarettes and Cheer detergent.

The logotype is also important. It, too, is vital in building a favorable brand image. Type faces or letters have symbolic meaning. Some lettering styles symbolize strength, some weakness; some say delicate, some denote roughness. Some are static and other styles suggest motion.

Easy readability is important. A brand name that is difficult to read is a deterrent in marketing. It has to symbolize the character of the product or the company. It has to be interesting and has to communicate literally and symbolically.

Still another factor in effective packaging is color. The color can also mean either marketing success or failure.

The right color combination is one that attracts attention and at the same time has appeal.

Because high preference colors have poor retention in the memory and those that have strong retention in the memory rate low in preference, colors frequently have to be used in pairs, usually in complementary pairs. One of the colors is to attract the eye and the other is to provide the appeal. In choosing a color, we must make sure that it does not have negative associations with the particular product. If possible, it is advisable to use a color that has favorable associations with the product.

In my books, *Color for Profit* and *Color Guide for Marketing Media*, I discuss the problems of color in detail.

The quality of the printing, particularly if appetite appeal is involved, is also of great importance in marketing. A poorly printed package is a poor marketing tool.

The present-day package is indeed complex. That is why the best designers have to be employed to develop packages that can be effective marketing tools.

However, the best designers cannot tell whether a package design will be an effective marketing tool. Packages are complex, and human beings still more complex. Designers are by nature, conditioning and training, the most complex individuals.

Certainly, designers are not typical consumers. Their tastes, preferences and ideas are not in keeping with those of the masses of consumers. They cannot be, because of the kind of personality, background and experience a designer must have in order to be able to create.

Therefore, research must be used to determine whether the design is an effective marketing tool. There is no one test that can provide this information because too many factors are involved. We must have tests that determine display effectiveness, attraction power, attention-holding power and brand name readability.

We must have tests that reveal consumer attitudes and actual preferences, or choices in which self-interest is involved. Mere interviews will not disclose such information. The tests have to be conducted on an unconscious level so that the respondents feel free to express their true attitudes and real feelings.

I have seen some of the most beautiful packages fail to pass an eye-movement test that measures eye-flow and attention-holding power.

I have seen some stunning packages that failed the readability test. In other words, the brand name or product name on the package was too difficult to read from the shelf.

Many appealing, aesthetically fine packages fail in the visibility test, which means that they are lost in the super market. They fail to attract attention.

There are packages that have great display effectiveness. They pass all three ocular tests—visibility, readability and eye-movement—but they fail in the association or preference tests.

A package that is effective in display, that has a high percentage of favorable associations and rates high in the preference test, is an effective marketing tool.

After the manufacturer of a consumer product knows he has a product of the right quality and an effective package, he should examine the advertising problem.

The Advertising

Advertising is the number three wall of a marketing structure. The kind and amount of advertising has much to do with the degree of success of any marketing program. Without doubt, the quantitative aspect of an advertising program is a major factor in any successful marketing. However, as I have pointed out, there are many instances in which the sheer weight of a large sum of money was not sufficient for producing a successful marketing program.

The qualitative aspect of advertising is at least as important as the quantitative one. No one will deny that the character of the campaign, the nature of the marketing theme, the type of printed ads and kind of filmed commercials have much to do with the success or failure of a marketing program.

Ad agencies have "copy geniuses," men and women who have a natural or acquired ability to create unusual advertising copy. Like most geniuses, like most creative people, they often talk to their own kind, not to the general public. Many ad agency executives are aware that printed ads and filmed commercials have to be tested with potential consumers to determine their marketing effectiveness. And how do most of them test the printed ads and filmed commercials? They use "playbacks" or "recognition" tests. Such tests are conducted on the assumption that printed ads and filmed commercials affect people, only on a conscious level.

Studies that have been conducted in the last twelve years show conclusively that individuals are influenced by advertising without being aware of that influence. An individual is motivated to buy something by an ad, but he often does not know what motivated him.

Most advertising agencies plan all advertising on the assumption that printed ads and filmed commercials affect consumers only on a conscious level. That is why they measure the effectiveness of ads by means of "playbacks" or "recognition" tests. The ad that is recalled or recognized by the greatest number of potential consumers is considered the best ad. Filmed commercials are tested on the same general principle.

I have known a number of advertising campaigns consisting of ads with high "retention" and "recognition" scores that have failed^ Neither the agency nor the client could understand why the campaign was a flop. The fact that the ads antagonized people did not enter their minds.

That consumers had unfavorable attitudes toward the ads did not occur to them. That the ads did not motivate people to buy had no meaning. They were impressed only with the fact that a carefully chosen sample of potential consumers of the product remembered the ad once they had seen it and could recognize the filmed commercial after viewing it once.

Since most people are not always conscious of having seen an ad, billboard or filmed commercial, they cannot always tell about it in an interview. Thus, the most effective, the most motivating experimental ads may have been discarded because they were not remembered or recognized by most of the respondents.

We have conducted many tests in the last dozen years showing conclusively that people have to be motivated to remember objects or ads and have to be motivated to buy a specific product. Over ten years ago I reported experiments showing conclusively that ads have much more effect on the unconscious mind than on the conscious.

We have much evidence that for advertising to be effective, it must not merely tell people to buy the product, it must motivate them to buy it. For an ad to be motivating, it must be pleasing, not irritating. It must have favorable connotations and pleasant associations.

How do we determine the effectiveness of an ad if not by "playback" and "recognition" tests? We have a number of tests, each of which shows one aspect of effectiveness.

First we put the ad through an eye-movement test that shows how the eyes travel over the ad and where attention is held. If this test is favorable, then the ad is put through two types of association tests, one that shows consumers' attitudes toward the ad and another that discloses whether the ad upgrades or downgrades the product. The second test is conducted because the ad is not supposed to sell itself. It has to sell the product. In conjunction with the association test, we have an indirect preference test that shows actual preference, consumer action in which self-interest is involved.

We don't want to know merely whether the potential consumers remember the ad. We want to find out whether the ad makes the potential consumer favorably disposed toward the product. We want to know whether it motivates the potential consumer to buy the product.

Price

The fourth side or wall of a marketing structure is price. The average consumer assumes that price is based on cost. We all know that the manufacturer must consider a multitude of factors in determining the price. He has to add up the cost of producing, promoting and selling the article before he can establish its retail price. Here I want to discuss an often neglected factor in pricing, the psychological factor.

Before going further into the discussion of pricing, we should divide all merchandise into necessities and luxuries. These are broad classifications which are important elements in pricing.

Seasonal vegetables and fruits are necessities. The same produce, out of season, is a luxury. In June, strawberries can be considered as a necessary food, but in January, strawberries are definitely a luxury. Meat is a necessity; steak is a luxury. Fish from a nearby body of water should not be classified as a luxury. Sea fish on the coast is not a luxury. Any food that has no more nutritional value than a less costly food should be classified as a luxury.

Commodities that are necessary for daily living are highly competitive and, at best, are profitable only because they are sold in large volume. Pricing of staples is almost entirely based on cost plus a small margin of profit per unit. Retail prices of common foods and other necessities in communities of unskilled workers whose incomes are minimal can be set primarily on two considerations, cost and competition.

In the United States, in communities where the standard of living is generally high, luxuries become necessities, psychological satisfactions become needs and emotional factors become daily habits.

In primitive and agricultural societies, symbolism played a major role only in religion. In our present-day, highly industrialized society, symbolism plays a vital role in almost every aspect of life.

Most people buy symbols, not products. Consumers generally know little about the actual quality of the product. They buy the image of the product, the image that is inspired by the brand name, the brand-identifying image, the label, the printed advertising, the filmed commercials and the publicity about the product or company that makes it.

A man buys a Chevrolet, Ford or Plymouth for transportation, but he gets a Cadillac, Lincoln or Imperial for other reasons, mainly psychological reasons. The luxury car is a class symbol. It is a prestige identification element. It provides ego satisfaction. It has social status.

LOUIS CHESKIN

The ego-involvement and prestige identification in owning a luxury car are not often admitted by the owner. Generally, the owner is not aware of the psychological reasons for getting a luxury car. If you ask a man why he drives a Cadillac or a Lincoln Continental, he will nearly always try to give you practical reasons. He will point out the safety features and even economy. He will normally say nothing about the ego satisfaction, the prestige symbolism and the social status it gives him.

Because consumers know little about most products, they look for labels, trademarks and brand names in the super market, the drug store, hardware store and in the department store.

Price is a major factor in the "quality image." To the consumer, a high quality product is a costly product. A fine article is an expensive article.

To most consumers, poor quality and low price are synonymous. When a woman says this is a cheap garment, she usually means that it is both poor in quality and low in price.

Price, like the package, is a psychological factor. High price is a symbol of status and is associated with prestige. High price and an expensive looking package are the necessary marketing twins for articles that are commonly used as gifts by the upper middle classes. The package has to express the price. To have status, an article has to look expensive and be expensive.

Many a product failed because the package or the product styling looked cheap and the price was too low. Of course, many products also fail because they are too high in price for the particular strata of consumers for which the product is intended.

The market for the product is an important factor in pricing. If the product is to be sold to consumers in the lowest economic strata, the lower the price the greater the volume of sales there will be. If the product is intended for executives, it is generally advisable to have the most attractive packaging with a high retail price.

In some communities, there are shoppers who will not buy an object because it is priced too low. In other communities, shoppers will not buy the product or cannot afford to buy it because it is priced too high.

Articles that are commonly bought to be used as gifts have to be priced in keeping with the gift concepts of the particular class of consumer. For some markets a typical gift is a $2 or $3 article. In others, a gift is generally from $5 to $10, and for some special markets, gifts range from $25 to $100 and more. Gifts are status symbols.

Price, the fourth side of profit is as complex as the other three because it too involves psychological as well as practical elements. The right price of the particular product for a specific class of consumers is vital in successful marketing. The price is a status symbol.

How do we know whether the product or article is priced right? The answer is by testing. We have founds that the ideal way is for the consumers to decide the price. Tests conducted with potential consumers, on an unconscious level, show clearly what the right price is for the product. I have seen many examples in which consumers priced an article higher than the actual price. I have seen cases in which consumers priced a product much lower than the actual price.

In one test most consumers priced a set of dishes at $35, whereas the manufacturer was going to have it retailed at $24.50. Another set of dishes was to have a retail price of $45, but a large majority of consumers in controlled tests priced it at $29.50. This part of the test in itself indicated that the set of dishes was overpriced for the market and the marketing program would not be a success.

I recall a study of ladies' sports clothes that were to be sold at $7.50 and $12.50. In this test, consumers priced the articles the opposite way. They thought the $7.50 articles were superior to the $12.50 ones, and they priced them accordingly.

In another study, four grades of men's shoes were tested. The retail prices were $12.50, $17.50, $19.50 and $24.50. A large majority of consumers thought the $17.50 shoes were the best and the $19.50 ones were second best.

Determining the consumers' idea of the price of the article is one way of measuring the marketability of the product. The shopper likes to feel that he is getting the maximum value for his money. Often, the best quality does not look like the best to the shopper.

Product tests that are conducted at the Color Research Institute are designed so that they reveal three marketing aspects; 1—consumer attitudes, 2—price evaluation and 3—actual preference.

The Four Sides

Product quality is the number one side in a profitable marketing program, the *package* is the number two side, *advertising* is the number three side and *pricing* is number four. Actually, a marketing program depends on all four, equally. Weakness of any one of the four sides will cut sales and diminish profits.

The total brand image in the mind of the consumer is the key to successful marketing. The XYZ Company is not selling vegetables, it is selling XYZ vegetables. The ABC fruit grower's corporation is not selling fruit, it is selling ABC fruit, which is no ordinary fruit.

The fruit stand on the highway is there to make sales. The farmer sets up a fruit stand and hopes to attract many of the travelers who happen to drive by the stand. A company cannot grow merely by making sales. A company must make customers. The growth of a company depends on building brand loyalty and making repeat sales.

Products such as fruit, fish and meat obviously cannot be identified with a company or brand by the styling, form or design of the product. Such products can only be given brand character by labeling or packaging.

For the label or package to have maximum marketing effectiveness, it has to have an appealing brand name, a psychologically meaningful brand-identifying image or symbol, an easy to read logotype and optically and psychologically correct color. The label or package as a whole has to have display effectiveness and favorable connotations.

The package is a basic factor in the total brand image, and the brand name and brand-identifying image are the basic elements of the package. The package is the visual manifestation of the product or brand. It symbolizes the character of the product or brand.

For the package to have the greatest effectiveness in building brand loyalty, it must be supported by a product better than that of competition, or at least as good.

The brand-identifying image and the package should always be incorporated into all advertising and promotion material.

The price should be in accordance with the class of consumer and the "quality image" of the product.

The product, the package, the advertising and the price have to be coordinated into one image, into a single entity and into a unified effect.

It is not possible for management to be in the position of a typical consumer. The character of management is totally different from that of the consumer. Most executives do not live, feel, and act like typical consumers and they cannot predict how consumers will behave.

Much business is still conducted on the basis of hunches. We hear about those who rose to the top because they made the right marketing decisions. Most wrong business decisions are never heard of. Running a business on hunches is a precarious business in these highly competitive times.

Necessity is the mother of invention. Because of the great growth of competitive enterprise, marketing research was given impetus. Much progress has been made in marketing research in recent years. We no longer need to rely on hunches and hope that we have guessed right about how consumers will react to a new product.

Modern research can get for us the answer to every marketing problem. Great strides have been made in the field of psychology, and the techniques from the field of psychology are being applied to marketing research. Tests that are conducted on an unconscious level reveal the true attitudes of consumers and disclose real preferences.

In modern research, we do not rely on what people say about a new product, a new package, a new brand-identifying image, a new brand name or about an ad or a filmed commercial.

We know now that people cannot or will not tell how they feel about a product. Usually they are not aware how they feel about the matter. Often, they think they know, but believe that they should not tell for a number of psychological reasons. The respondent in an interview normally wants to make a favorable impression. He desires to be fashionable or pleasant. All sorts of defense mechanisms come into play in an interview.

However, in tests that are conducted on an unconscious level, the respondents are not aware of what is being tested. The tests are structured; controls are built into them. The tests are designed and conducted so that the representative individuals in the consumer test respond naturally, spontaneously, and reveal their real feelings and true attitudes.

Tests conducted on an unconscious level are being used for measuring the effectiveness of all sides of the marketing structure—product, package, advertising and price— and for determining the marketing potential of the total marketing program.

In order to use modern methods for predetermining the marketing effectiveness of a marketing tool or a new product, we must free ourselves from past practices of conducting business on the basis of hunches and open our minds to the new ways, to the new techniques and procedures for solving present-day marketing problems.

Those who have vested interests in the old ways, in the old research methods, are resisting the new research techniques. They try to confuse, to mislead and throw suspicion on the new methods. In every field the old resists the new. This is in the nature of life itself.

Those of us who are alert and progressive do not fear the new. We open our eyes and minds and examine the facts objectively, coolly, without preconceived notions and without prejudice.

The techniques of testing on an unconscious level were introduced into the marketing field in September of 1944. I trace the history and progress of unconscious level testing in my book, *How to Predict What People Will Buy*, which was published in September, 1957. I outline the techniques used, and report on the marketing successes that confirmed the findings of the tests. I tell about the research that was done on Good Luck margarine and Lux soap, both products of Lever Brothers, Marlboro cigarettes, Bissel sweepers and many other well-known brands.

My main objective here, however, is not only to outline the interdependence of the four sides—product, package, advertising and pricing—in supporting a healthy, profitable marketing program, but to go deeper into the scientific, psychological, unconscious-level factors in marketing.

CHAPTER 3

IMAGERY AND COLOR IN PACKAGING

EACH HUE, tint, shade or tone has a specific optical and psychological effect. A color occupies area or space and is generally part of an image. The psychological impression the image makes depends greatly on the color, because the color is a vital component of the image.

The image on a package may be simple or complex. It may be a basic geometric shape or an intricate design, or an illustration of an animate or inanimate object. It may consist of a combination of various types of elements. Simple or complex, with or without color, it serves as a symbol. It identifies the package or brand and characterizes and classifies it by its symbolism.

Often, the image symbolizes the company as a whole and serves as the focal point of the entire company image. It performs as the hub of the company identity to the consumer and is a trademark that may have favorable or unfavorable connotations.

All the elements that characterize the company and everything that is related to it constitute the total company image. The pivotal point of the total company image is a basic image or trademark which performs as a symbol.

The total company image comprises a symbolic image or trademark, a color or several colors, the architecture of the building in which the company is housed, the character of the advertising, the kind of press comments about the company and the manner in which the company performs its services or delivers its goods. The symbolic image, generally, is the key to the total company image.

The symbol for a company image may be a crest, shield, geometric shape, color (of the product or the label), abstract design, realistic image, banner or monogram.

The image on a package becomes identified with the package and thus the package becomes the symbol that may have favorable or unfavorable connotations. The package communicates the character and/or quality of the product.

Research conducted on an unconscious level and marketing experience of recent years have shown that we are all greatly influenced by symbols. We are usually motivated by the image of an idea rather than by the idea itself. Book jackets motivate us to buy some books and labels motivate us to buy certain brands of food, soap, etc. In the super market we make choices on the basis of the visual effect. Unconsciously, we transfer the effect from the exterior of the package to the contents. We are guided by the symbol in making choices without realizing what actually motivates us in accepting one article instead of another.

Sensation transference is a common occurrence in the super market. Acceptance or rejection of a product or brand is often brought about by the package. If the label symbolizes high quality, consumers assume that the product is of high quality. If the label (design or color) symbolizes low quality, consumers transfer the "low quality" effect of the label to the product itself.

Research shows that consciously we assign no importance to symbols, but unconsciously we are deeply affected by them. The psychological powers of basic images and colors are difficult for most people to comprehend fully, because these powers operate in the realm of the unconscious.

We cannot make an objective evaluation of an image or a color because we are not conscious of its effect upon us. We are not aware whether it affects us favorably or unfavorably. We cannot generally tell whether it has any effect on us at all.

First research and later marketing experience has shown that, although we are influenced by the image of quality more than by the actual quality of the product, a quality image by itself is not enough for successful marketing. Our tests have shown that a quality image must be backed up by a quality product. It can be built and maintained only if it is supported by a quality product.

The quality image plays the primary role in the first sale. For repeat sales, actual product quality is as important as the image of quality.

Recently, the public has become aware of false symbols. In the year 1958, consumers began making choices that are to a considerable degree more rational than they were a few years back.

Our present sober attitudes can be traced to the psychological shock we received from the Sputniks and satellites and there is evidence that the effect of the first shock has been aggravated by our awareness of hydrogen bombs and intercontinental and cosmic rockets and by our own Atlas.

Our clients are no longer concerned only with images, packages, brand names and marketing themes for new products. We are now being asked to determine the consumers' attitudes toward the product itself before proceeding with the tests of the brand-identifying image, package, brand name and marketing theme.

For successful marketing, an effective package with an appealing brand-identifying symbol always has to express the quality, because all humans judge a book by its cover, coffee by the container and a man by the clothes he wears.

Although some believe otherwise, we have evidence that women are much more attractive with clothes than without. The clothes must be right in design and in color for the particular woman. The package design must be right for the specific product. This means that package designers and stylists will always be with us.

They are generally artists who combine creativity with practical elements. They correlate the aesthetic with the functional and deal with physical and psychological factors. They are subjective in expression and character, yet strive to communicate. Originality is the designer's greatest asset, yet he seeks to reach an audience that has been conditioned to old forms.

Because people feel secure with the old and the familiar, they resist the original and the new. Although people resist the completely new idea or form, they are also bored or unstimulated by anything that is old and familiar.

The conflicting attitudes toward the old or familiar and the original or new make product, and package designing a complex psychological problem. Almost every original design consists of diverse and often psychologically clashing elements. Few things are either black or white. There are numerous tones, tints and shades, each with its kind and degree of effect. There are many degrees of newness.

Research has shown and experience has confirmed that in design, as in most matters, something new about the old has the greatest acceptance, because the new aspect is stimulating and interesting and the old element makes one feel secure and confident.

How much of the old and how much new should an object have in order to have maximum acceptance? This question can be answered by research that probes unconscious motives.

Some researchers and package designers have said that only the whole, the complete package, should be tested, not parts. This statement stems from a superficial familiarity with Gestalt psychology. The basic Gestalt psychology principle is that the whole is more or less than the sum of its parts. It also stresses that each part must be healthy and effective, that one weak component weakens the whole. It stresses interdependence of the parts and emphasizes organization and coordination of the parts, but it does not disregard the parts.

Parts of a package are tested as well as the whole, because the whole depends on its parts. The whole can be weakened by one weak part. A poor brand-identifying image can weaken the effectiveness of a brand. The wrong color can cut sales. A logo of poor readability can hinder marketing progress. Each component part must be tested separately in order to ascertain its effectiveness, to find out whether it is vital to the whole, or whether it should be slightly modified or eliminated.

The whole must be tested because the effectiveness of the whole package depends on the arrangement of the parts.

The "visual effectiveness" of the whole is determined by an eye-movement test. The psychological effect of the whole is revealed in a field test conducted on an unconscious level with several hundred consumers.

The procedure for determining the marketing effectiveness of a package or ad can be compared with determining the health of a person. First the doctor examines or tests the heart, lungs, eyes, etc. He then proceeds to determine the functioning of the entire nervous system and psychological behavior.

We know now that an individual's habits cannot be changed easily. His behavior is conditioned by heredity, early upbringing, the kind and degree of parental love and affection, education, environment, social pressures and economic status. Men and women have strong likes and dislikes and often deep-seated fetishes and phobias. Some have abnormal attachments to particular colors or images. Others have abnormally strong dislikes for certain colors or shapes. Most normal people do not have extreme aversions (phobias) or abnormal attachments (fetishes) to objects. But people differ in their preferences. Each reacts to an object according to his own make-up. Some objects have wide appeal, other articles, images or colors appeal to a minority.

Some attitudes in individuals are almost impossible to change. Prejudices are very difficult to eradicate and new ideas are acceptable to most people, only if they are not in conflict with deep-seated habits or concepts.

A glaring fallacy in the marketing field is the assumption that a big advertising campaign can condition people to accept anything. Many advertising specialists believe that marketing success depends primarily on the coverage and saturation of the advertising. Motivation studies, or more precisely, tests conducted on an unconscious level, show that some attitudes cannot be changed by an advertising program, no matter how extensive it is.

We know that consumers make some rational choices. They can generally differentiate between an inferior and a superior product.

However, choices are made emotionally, much more frequently than rationally. Shoppers are motivated by symbols, by images and/or colors. Sensation transference from the design on the package to the product in the package plays a major role in the super market. This role is frequently a decisive one in a marketing program.

CHAPTER 4

AUTO MAKERS' PROBLEMS CAN BE SOLVED

AN AUTO manufacturing organization is a carefully planned, efficiently run operation. It has to be. Mass production is not possible without planning, without organization and coordination of the various production departments. Technical problems that are related to production are given careful attention. Parts that go into the composition of the car and finally the complete car are carefully tested.

However, the prospective buyers of cars are given either little attention or the wrong kind of attention. Evidently, cars are produced without giving consideration to the economic status of car buyers or to the psychological needs and wants of Americans.

This lack of recognition of the consumers' needs is clearly illustrated by the trend in making all cars bigger every year. A few years ago Cadillac was the big G.M. luxury car; Buick was the big, efficient car; Oldsmobile was the big car with innovations or new gadgets every year; Pontiac was the heavy duty car and Chevrolet was the small, economy car. Although each make had several models in a number of price ranges, those were the basic consumer classifications. (Recent studies show that many car owners still classify the cars in this way.)

Now the Chevrolet is not much smaller than a Cadillac and when fully equipped has almost all the luxuries of a Cadillac. The price is almost as high as of the lowest priced Cadillac. It is higher than that of the lowest priced Buick, Oldsmobile or Pontiac.

Ford had the Lincoln, the Mercury and the Ford. The first was the luxury liner, the second the middle class car and the third the economy car. Now you can buy a Ford fully equipped that costs more than a Mercury.

The Thunderbird is sold by Ford dealers, is made in the Lincoln plant and has a price tag, when fully equipped, nearly as high as a Lincoln and as high or higher than a Mercury.

The Plymouth is almost as luxurious and really no smaller than the Chrysler. DeSoto and Dodge have lost their class distinctions.

The auto makers themselves have thus for several years been in the process of destroying the automobile's role as a status symbol. They have been gradually undermining the status symbolism of cars by upgrading the so-called low priced car every year so that it has just as much of an image of "quality" and "size" as the big car or the luxury car.

There seems to have been competition between the lowest and highest price cars as to which can have more chrome ornamentation and the greatest number of gadgets. In 1958 there was little real difference between the Cadillac and the Chevrolet. Buick won the prize, however, for having the most gaudy and most offensive chrome ornamentation.

Obviously, many 1959 cars were designed on the premise that exaggerated fins are more important than storage space, comfort or even safety. However, gaudy chrome and garish multiple colors have been eliminated.

Because of the recent great social changes, attitudes of Americans have changed. Those of high income, as well as low, refused to pay for worthless, elaborate chrome. In 1958, the automobile manufacturers could see clearly that there was a large demand for smaller cars. They also learned that, in the near future, cars will have to be still simpler and more functional.

However, there is evidence that the auto makers still don't

know how to find out how car buyers will react to a specific car design.

Top management is concerned with every step of the development of a new car design. Much time is consumed in the making of management decisions. All sorts of problems are involved which have to be solved by management. These problems are not known to the average car buyer.

For marketing strategy, cars have to have "family resemblance." All General Motors cars have to look like General Motors cars. All Ford cars have to look like they belong to the Ford family of cars. The same is true of Chrysler and American Motors. The Chevrolet and Cadillac have to have some things in common, but not the Chevrolet and Ford or the Cadillac and Lincoln.

Each car model must also have its own character and identity. A Ford must not look like a Mercury. A Pontiac must not be mistaken for a Chevrolet.

Designers make sketches of car details. They create designs of fenders, grilles, lights, bumpers, etc. They make numerous sketches of complete cars. A dozen or more of the sketches are chosen and are produced full size. The Product Planning group eliminates many of the full size sketches.

Six to ten full size sketches are presented to the men in top management who decide which of the designs are worth giving serious consideration. These are made into full size clay models. It takes almost six months to produce the clay models.

At this stage the engineers are called into the styling department. Now they begin to do some thinking about their problems, about fitting the functional elements into the design created by the stylists.

Meanwhile, some of the design features leak to competition and reports also come in about what competitive companies are doing with their styling. This usually means more changes.

Each new model must have specific identity. Each car design must have recognition features in the grille, fenders, fins, etc. A competitor's car having the same details or recognition elements can lead to marketing disaster.

The styling has to conform to engineering factors and comfort needs in the car interior. While the stylists are busy with their problems, the engineers have been in the process of producing a mechanical prototype.

In the entire American auto manufacturing industry, members of top management make design decisions. They obviously make judgments on the styling, on the basis of their personal feelings. The executives merely have to agree among themselves on which design should be put into production.

Members of top management decide, twelve to fourteen months before new model introduction time, which of the three or four clay models is the kind of design that the public will like best. They may select one of the three models as is or decide to see a model made up of elements from two or more of the designs.

The group making the decision generally consists of the president, general manager, vice presidents in charge of sales, manufacturing and finance and the chief stylist.

If a Sputnik, cosmic rocket or Atlas appears on the world scene and brings about a great change in public taste or in consumer preference, nothing can be done in Detroit to change the design to meet the new consumer demand. The best they can do, they believe, is to insist that there really is no change in public demand, that the American people really want the kind of cars that Detroit is producing.

Obviously, not much can be done in Detroit about Sputniks, hydrogen bombs and intercontinental missiles. However, much can be done about determining consumer attitudes toward various designs under normal social and economic conditions.

Top management in the auto industry knows now that people buy styling, not performance, because they take the performance of a car for granted. Yet, it does not recognize that styling is involved with deep psychological elements. In the auto industry the men who decide what should be produced and put on the market don't seem to be aware that a person's background, environment, social and economic status have much to do with design preference. These industrial leaders seem to disregard the fact that they are not typical car buyers and, therefore, cannot possibly react to car designs like typical car buyers. Perhaps they are aware of this but do not know what to do about it, without the risk of revealing designs to competition.

When Detroit does request market research, it is the kind that shows what people say, not what they really want. The research also is of abstract ideas about cars, not of the actual car designs.

All 1958 cars suffered from the drastic psychological change in the American people that was primarily brought about by the Sputniks. However, tests show that the 1958 Edsel suffered mainly from basic design weaknesses. Studies conducted on an unconscious level disclosed that the first Edsel lacked an image of modernity and had some strong negative associations. The studies showed that a large percentage of car owners associated the Edsel car design with a 1935 model and the car suggested lack of power and stability.

Marketing research could not predict the Sputniks and the recession, but the right kind of marketing research could have revealed the negative elements in the Edsel car design. Because of the policy of complete secrecy, the car design had not been tested at all, according to reliable reports.

The Edsel marketing plan suffered from the fact that the car was launched on the assumption that the car design is not as important a factor in marketing as the image that advertising and publicity can create.

Also, the name of the new car, obviously, was not chosen on the basis of research, but for sentimental reasons. Almost every aspect of the promotion and advertising was researched extensively, although quantitatively more than qualitatively, but not the car itself or the name.

An illuminating comparison in the automotive marketing field is that of the 1958 Thunderbird and the 1958 Edsel. The four seater Thunderbird was not launched with great fanfare nor with a huge advertising campaign. In spite of the mild promotion and comparatively small advertising budget, the Thunderbird became a great success. It was not touched by the recession or the Sputniks, or affected by the slump in car buying. It continued to be in great demand until the 1959 model came out, for which there was continued demand.

Research that was conducted on an unconscious level, experimentally, showed why. The tests revealed that consumer attitudes toward the design were highly favorable and the name, Thunderbird, harmonized with the car design. They showed that the name had great appeal, that the car design had great appeal and that the combination of the name and the design appealed to the public.

Managers in Detroit have finally become aware that they do not know what the consumers want. This they could have known by studying the behavioral sciences. Executives of large corporations should at this stage of our national development realize that they cannot possibly behave like typical consumers, or react like typical consumers, for the simple reason that they are not typical consumers.

Some of the auto makers have at last decided that they have to go to the public for guidance. How are they getting the guidance? They have arranged for representatives of the public to judge the new models.

Detroit still has not found out that people cannot or will not tell you directly what they want in a car or why they really like a car or anything else. It still does not seem to know about testing on an unconscious level.

Evidently they still are not aware in Detroit that people cannot or will not say what their real, deep feelings are.

The Detroit manufacturers' insistence that the necessity for keeping car designs secret would make any kind of design testing impossible is no longer true. The fact that it takes more than two years to complete a car design is no reason for not testing. It is not true that the public taste in design changes in two or three years, as some in Detroit claim. Quite to the contrary, studies show that under normal social and economic conditions the public resists change and rejects radical change.

New toiletries, new food products, soaps and many other types of articles also take over two years to get to the market. Most of the products that we handle take two years and more to reach the market. It takes from three months to a year to develop the product to meet quality standards. It then takes from six months to a year to get package designs created and tested and from six months to a year to develop a marketing program and advertising theme and another three months to test them. Finally, another two or three months are needed to produce the product, the packages, the promotional material and the ads.

It is true that people normally want something new about the old. They reject the completely new and original and they are bored by the old and familiar.

We also know that we are witnessing the first major change in public taste in seven years. We had been getting the same responses to a number of designs in the last half dozen years. For the first time, the consumer responses to these designs are completely different.

Detroit deals mainly with steel for making cars. Other manufacturers use organic and inorganic ingredients to produce products for super markets and drug stores. Producers of all commodities are confronted with similar problems because they all produce for the same people and for the same market. The consumer is the basis of every marketing problem.

We have conclusive evidence that management does not and cannot know what the consumers want. What is even more baffling to individuals with traditional marketing concepts, is that the consumer himself cannot or will not tell what he wants.

There are psychological reasons why asking people what kind

of cars they want will not produce the answers. The following are some typical responses.

When a man (or woman) is asked what kind of a new model car he would like to have, he gives rational answers. He gives practical answers. He says he wants a reliable car, a safe car, a powerful car with fast pickup or an economical car. But when he says he wants both power and economy, he wants to eat his cake and have it too.

Most individuals, in the process of buying a car, are rarely rational. Our tests show that most buyers of cars actually do not know why they buy a particular car. Tests conducted on an unconscious level reveal that a number of people bought cars because of a certain curve in the styling. Others bought cars because the steering wheel fascinated them. A number bought a certain make of car because they were deeply affected by the dashboard. Others bought cars because the colors appealed to them. Still others bought a brand of car because the name of the car had deep meaning to them.

When the reasons for buying the cars were pointed out to the respondents in the tests, almost all of them denied these were the reasons. With few exceptions, each one insisted that he bought the car for rational reasons.

This behavior in relation to cars does not appear to be so surprising if we are aware that many a young man marries a girl because he loves her cute nose, her blonde hair or a specific part of her anatomy.

There is no doubt that in the super market most purchases are irrationally motivated. The following two examples are well known in marketing circles. When we gave housewives three packages of coffee, almost 90% of them told us that one of the three is a far superior product to the other two. Actually, only the containers differed. When we served yellow margarine and white butter at luncheons, the guests enjoyed the yellow-colored pat, but they could not stand the oily, flat taste of the little white squares.

LOUIS CHESKIN

Most people actually believe that they are rational individuals. They really are not aware that they are emotional creatures, impulsive or compulsive. Usually, they are sincere in giving rational reasons for making purchases.

We have all been taught since early childhood to behave in a rational manner, and we strive to be logical and practical. But most of the time we lose this battle in our daily living, working, loving and buying.

There are the others, who do not want to give the true answers. They consciously give answers which they know or think are untrue. They justify this misrepresentation in the belief that their feelings about matters of taste are personal and private.

Elements of "ego-involvement" and "prestige identification" play their roles in all interviews. The respondent wants to give the impression of being intelligent, practical, fashionable or merely pleasant and for one or more of these reasons will not reveal his real feelings or true attitudes.

When we asked a number of persons what kind of magazines they subscribed to, most of them gave the names of prestige publications, few mentioned *True Story* magazine. The actual subscription list showed that *True Story* magazine and a number of other pulp publications had by far the largest subscriptions.

Recent tests with car owners revealed that when the owners of foreign-made cars were asked why they bought the cars, almost all of them gave economy as the reason. Every auto maker has stripped models which can be bought for from $500 to $1,500 less than fully equipped models, but these basic cars which provide just as good transportation as the fully equipped autos, do not sell. Americans don't want them for a number of practical and psychological reasons.

A study of why many buy foreign-made cars revealed that the reasons are not altogether rational. The study shows that economy is one reason, but not at all the most important one. Much more motivating are that the foreign cars are "cute," "different," "unusual" and "distinctive." Those who can afford the high prices buy the large imported cars. Those with limited incomes buy the low-cost makes and still have the gratification of being "different," "original" or "unique." The study shows that most of the individuals who buy the small foreign cars, selling at $1,700 to $2,700, would not want to be seen in an economy model Plymouth, Ford or Chevrolet, minus radio, directional signals, cigarette lighters, white-wall tires, power steering and power brakes.

However, the buyers of the 1958 Rambler, Thunderbird and Lincoln represent still three other segments of the American car buyer, who have one thing in common. They were all repelled by the gaudiness and juke-box effect of most of the other 1958 cars.

Rambler buyers are individuals who have to or want to be practical. They buy cars, perhaps also other products, for practical reasons.

How about the buyer of a Thunderbird? He buys the car because of its character, not merely because of its performance or even because of the comfort it provides, but for its total Thunderbird character.

When a man buys a Lincoln, he does not want merely a big, luxurious car. He buys it because the Lincoln has a specific image, a character that differs from the image and character of a Cadillac or a Chrysler. When a man buys a Cadillac he is not merely buying transportation.

People buy cars to fit their pocketbooks and their personalities. Men and women buy almost all products for both reasons. People expect the house they buy to keep out the rain and cold. But they do not buy the house for this basic reason. Nor does one buy clothes merely to keep warm or for reasons of modesty alone. Appearance, design, color, style and fashion play major roles in the selection of all products in a highly developed industrial society like ours.

The shortage of parking space in large cities is a practical reason why small cars will be more and more in demand. As long as America has an economy of abundance, most Americans will not buy cars merely for transportation. For those Americans who want cars for transportation at low cost, there are the basic Ford, Chevrolet, Plymouth, Studebaker Scotsman or Lark and the Rambler.

The inexpensive American cars are much safer than the tiny imported models and are much more comfortable.

Motivation research came into being because people will not or cannot tell us what they really want. Only by testing with potential car buyers on an unconscious level can we find out what kind of car designs really appeal to the people.

Motivation research is needed because the person who buys a foreign-made car won't tell you that he bought the foreign-made car, instead of a stripped down, economical American product, because it has snob appeal, individuality and originality, because he wanted to be different from the common American car owner and could do it at no greater cost.

Motivation research studies have shown and marketing experience has confirmed that people declared one product superior to another in quality or in performance, although actually the two products differed only in styling or in packaging.

Motivation research has to be used because people are not aware of their actual reasons for buying cars or almost all other things, and cannot tell us why they like one design or style and not another. We must use unconscious level tests in order to find out their attitudes and to determine what actually motivates them.

Detroit's problems can be solved by merely making use of the modern research, by getting guidance and confirmation from tests that reveal true attitudes of car buyers. Tests that are conducted on an unconscious level disclose the real feelings. They are designed and conducted so that the respondents express themselves spontaneously, without being aware that they are revealing their attitudes.

A control test is used for taking the emphasis away from the object that is really being tested. The control test is planned to be of particular interest to the respondents. Controlled association-type tests that are integrated with objects of interest to the respondents do not bring out defense mechanisms in the respondents. They do not involve the respondent's ego. Prestige factors do not get into the testing situation. To get correct and true answers for Detroit we must use motivation research, indirect testing methods, not direct interviewing.

Controlled tests that are conducted on an unconscious level can reveal how much of the old and how much that is new a car should have in order to have maximum acceptance.

How can the tests be conducted without revealing the designs to competition? Actually, the answer is that secrecy is in the nature of motivation research itself. The procedure of testing on an unconscious level is based on secrecy.

Motivation studies show clearly that people often buy cars because specific details appeal to them. They like either the dashboard, or fenders, or bumpers, etc. Conversely, they often do not buy a car because they react negatively to a detail. They don't like the grille, the fenders, the bumpers or the interior styling. For this reason, it is necessary to test car parts before testing the whole.

A dozen, two dozen or even more, drawings of grille designs should be tested. Two, three or four of these grille designs will come out best in the tests.

The same type of tests should be conducted with designs for fenders, bumpers, interiors, etc. In each case, two, three or several designs will come to the top in favorable associations and in preference.

Finally, a number of combinations of parts, or whole cars should be submitted to controlled association-type tests. Many combinations should be tested, several of which may become candidates for production.

Several car designs should be parts of all tests, merely as controls, as testing devices, not to be considered for actual production. This aspect is very important because it serves both as a control in the test situation and as a means of keeping competition off the track.

By conducting market tests on an unconscious level, by testing parts before finally testing complete car designs, and by including in these tests some designs as controls, we can get the answers for a car maker without revealing plans to competition.

CHAPTER 5

WHAT IS AND WHAT IS NOT PREDICTABLE

IN THE latter part of 1957 and first half of 1958 there was a great deal of talk in business circles about economic recession. However, we had evidence that it was not the economic recession that has had the greatest effect on the American people.

Studies show that the attitudes of the American people have changed drastically since October of 1957. Such a great psychological change could not have been caused by the mild economic depression.

As recently as the summer of 1957, studies showed that people reacted favorably to elaborate ornamentation, gaudy color combinations and functionless chrome trim on cars and other steel products, although the favorable attitudes were not generally admitted in direct interviews. Later studies showed that people were reacting unfavorably to such ostentatious ornamentation. The studies revealed that people who only a year before were attracted by frills now reacted unfavorably to functionless objects.

Studies conducted in 1958 showed that the American public wanted simple cars, minus elaborate trim, large cars or small ones, whatever the need, but cars that were simple and functional in design.

Fewer people were buying new cars in 1958. Almost the entire automotive industry became depressed. The Rambler and

Thunderbird, however, were doing well. (Note that one is a utility car, the second a sports or luxury car.) These two brands were relatively simple in design, minus elaborate ornamentation and almost devoid of functionless chrome.

The chemise or sack dress was an attempt (in my opinion, a perverted one) to meet the demand for simplicity. The fashion industry is more sensitive to the public's wants or needs than the automotive industry, although it does not know exactly how to meet the need.

On the basis of studies conducted in the latter part of 1957, I declared that simplicity should characterize automobile design and that the sober look, the dignified form, the basically functional gadget, the single color or truly two-tone color will be bought by the American public.

Our studies showed that flamboyant fins and gaudy color combinations would no longer sell cars; useless gadgets would not appeal to 1959 and 1960 shoppers.

What is the primary cause for this basic psychological change? The answer is the Sputniks! Not the economic recession, but the satellites drastically changed our attitudes toward many things and ideas. On October 4, 1957, the Russians shocked and bewildered us. Studies showed that the sudden realization that we are not the best and first in everything gave us an inferiority complex. The discovery, that while we were fussing with useless decorations, they were making satellites and intercontinental ballistic missiles, had a profound psychological effect on almost every American.

The Sputniks made us more serious, more practical but not more rational. In 1958, I have seen more signs of psychological, than of economic depression. The behavior of many still indicates a certain amount of desperation. The urging by some that we adopt communist methods in order to compete with Russia is irrational. The emphasis on physical science and willingness to neglect the humanities and the behavioral sciences in education is irrational.

In business circles there has been evidence of confusion and the attitudes of some business people had the marks of desperation. Desperation was exemplified in the way subliminal projection was widely publicized, accepted by many, welcomed by some, and caused panic in a number of groups.

In 1958, marketing literature was full of dramatics, hysteria and doubt. There was an awful lot of nonsense written and said about several vital aspects of marketing. We have witnessed irrational debates on motivation research. There appeared irrational statements about testing the whole, versus testing component parts, as if one excluded the other.

Over fourteen years of testing marketing tools on an unconscious level has shown that we can predict accurately, to which of a given number of designs or products the public will react most favorably, six months or a year later, even two or three years later, if socio-economic conditions remain about the same and consumer attitudes follow a normal pattern.

However, in the latter part of 1957, socio-economic conditions had changed. The consumer had been psychologically affected by powerful forces—the Sputniks, the economic recession and later by our own Atlas and the Russian cosmic rocket.

Since October 4, 1957, the day the first Sputnik was launched, every medium of communication, T.V., radio, newspapers and magazines, has been filled with satellites, hydrogen bomb dangers, intercontinental rockets and our inferiority in education. These have had a profound effect on the American public, a much greater and deeper effect than any advertising campaign, even the biggest, could possibly have. The effect of all this should be measured and evaluated. We should ascertain to what extent these psychologically disturbing factors have had an effect on marketing.

We had been retesting a number of designs and found that for some products, designs to which consumers reacted favorably in 1956, had not done well in the tests conducted in late 1957 and in 1958. We detected a drastic change in consumer attitudes, particularly toward products in the hard goods field.

However, marketing failures were not all caused by socio-economic changes. Many were due to lack of objective research, misuse of research, and a lack of realization of the kind of research that should be used for discovering the attitudes and true wants of consumers.

The Edsel

An article by E. B. Weiss appeared in the issue of March 10, 1958, of *Advertising Age*. Perhaps, it was no worse than articles on subliminal projection, Bridie Murphy or space ships from Mars. Mr. Weiss urged use of "disciplined intuition" instead of research and used Edsel as an example of the failure of research. Obviously, Mr. Weiss based his article on intuition, not facts.

The fact is that the sales manager of Edsel, whom Mr. Weiss was quoting, was not marketing a car that had been designed with the aid of research.

On March 11, 1958, I addressed the Public Relations Clinic in Chicago and on March 18, the Public Relations Society of America in Chicago. In these addresses I said that the automotive industry should find out the real wants of the American people instead of producing what they think the people want. I saw in a U.P. story on April 1 that President Eisenhower commented on this subject.

There was a great deal of talk about research in connection with the Edsel, very much indeed. But there really was no serious research.

I know from reliable sources that there was no styling research, no psychological testing of any kind—of the car design as a whole or of the vital parts. There was no research on the choice of a brand name. The reason always given for not testing is the necessity of not revealing marketing plans to competition. The actual reason is a lack of realization of what modem research can do.

Mr. Weiss said he believes that 50 per cent of new products fail when put on the market, and some think it is 70 to 80 per cent.

Mr. Weiss obviously has not kept up with the times. He evidently did not know that products that have been reliably and thoroughly researched from all aspects— product design, promotion and advertising—did not fail.

Mr. Weiss revealed in his article that he closed his mind to the facts when he compared the period from 1915 to 1930 with present marketing conditions. How about all the cars that failed since 1915? Did they fail because of research or lack of it? What was wrong with the intuition? Wasn't it disciplined? Perhaps, "disciplined intuition" kept Mr. Weiss from realizing that in 1915 a man bought a car for transportation. In these days, both Mr. and Mrs. do the buying of cars. They get a Rambler, Plymouth, Ford or Chevrolet for transportation around the suburbs, and a Lincoln, Chrysler or Cadillac for show or prestige—and a little, just a little, extra riding comfort.

In earlier years, consumption was mainly of a biological and material nature; in our present society of abundance, consumption is largely psychological. (Eating hamburger fills a biological need. Steak provides psychological satisfaction.)

We must measure the effects of "brand images" and test styling, because these are vital psychological factors in contemporary American life and, therefore, in present-day marketing.

Henry Ford had only the one problem of providing transportation at low cost. Initiative and know-how, plus the realization that the public wanted cheap transportation, brought success to Ford, not "instinct," not "intuition."

The new products in the 1920's did not have to compete with comparable products. The new products were not new brands, they were truly new products, not comparable to existing products. The Model T Ford competed with the horse and buggy, not with cars that performed about as well and were sold at a price as low as the Ford.

Some individuals use the word "research" loosely. They talk to a few dealers about an imaginary car and they call it research. They put some questions to a few car owners and that is called research. They send out several thousand letters about a theoretical new car, to which they get several hundred replies, indicating that everything in the letter is just dandy, and that is called research.

If this is research, the Edsel had research.

If Mr. Weiss used the word research in this sense, then he was right in saying that research was worthless.

I am sure that Mr. Weiss was right in saying that the next great trend will be to smaller cars, less powerful and with much less chrome. This was quite obvious when he wrote it. The trend was already here. I knew and said these things in the fall of 1957 because I got my information from research, from tests conducted on an unconscious level.

The major reasons for the marketing failure of the 1958 Edsel are the following:

1. The styling was not planned on the basis of research.
2. The product was not planned to meet a specific consumer need.
3. The company did not or could not take into account the psychological effect that the Russian satellites had on the American people. (This was an unpredictable and an unmeasurable factor.)
4. Because of the economic slump and "Sputnik fever," increasing numbers of consumers began to resent paying for purposeless gingerbread on all cars, including the Edsel.
5. The actual car did not confirm the great publicity build-up of an image of quality, modernity and unusualness. The real car image did not match the imaginary image the consumers had. There was great disappointment.

There were still other elements that lined up against the 1958 Edsel, but these five are among the major factors. Most of the reasons for failure could have been avoided by using the right kind of research. Actually, all the elements could have been predicted, except that of the Russian launching of Sputnik I on October 4, 1957.

There was nothing wrong with the 1958 Edsel car mechanically. It was a very efficient vehicle. In performance, it was as good a car in every way as competitively priced cars and, in many respects, better than some. But it did not have the image of up-to-dateness. It did not have the image that the consumer had received from the great promotion and publicity.

Research of competitive brands often provides vital information. One of our experimental tests with cars revealed that, when a well-known prestige car removed the functional elements from the rear fins, the fins, which for years were identified with this brand, lost much of their quality connotation. The fins were a symbol of high quality as long as they were associated with rear light signals. When the fins lost their functional role, they also lost the image of quality. The quality image of this car suffered further from the fact that other cars adopted similar non-functional fins.

Another factor that contributed to the deterioration of the quality image of this car was the removal of the frame in order to lower it to make it more eye-appealing. The lack of a frame suggests to some people a lack of safety. The frame may actually not be a safety factor at all, but psychologically some individuals associate lack of a frame with lack of safety.

Still another contribution to image deterioration was the obvious attempt of economy in some parts of the car. These economies, although trivial, were in contradiction to the image of "luxury" and "quality." For example, the trunk was lined with paper. The tests revealed that this minor element caused great damage to the "quality image." The lack of quality connotation in the trunk lining was transferred to the entire car.

Such findings could have been very useful to the manufacturer of the Edsel.

Motivation research deals with the unconscious mind, and as long as we have an economy of abundance in which brands are competing for the consumer's dollar, we need research into the unconscious motives of the consumers.

You have to be sure that your product has favorable psychological connotations before it is put on the market, because the actual product may be about the same in performance as a competing product.

A product with a "quality image" has the marketing advantage over a competitor with an equally good or efficient product that lacks a "quality image." Initially, consumers react to the image of the product because they know very little about the actual product.

The importance of a "quality image" is still not widely realized among marketing people. However, there has been too much dependence recently on "quality image" in some quarters. They know, or will soon find out, that a "quality image" can be built and maintained only around a quality product.

I predict that in the not distant future we will have only big luxury cars, station wagons, sports cars and a predominance of small utility cars. I made this prediction before and I do not hesitate to repeat it. It is a prediction based on research.

Many suburban families will have two cars, one big luxury car or big station wagon (depending on financial and professional status), and one small car like the Rambler, that is economical to operate, for getting around town, for shopping and as a second car for the wife when the husband uses the big car. The sports car, such as the Thunderbird, will be popular with young sportsmen and older men and women who are young in spirit.

Because of the parking space problem, the small car will continue for some time to gain preference among urban dwellers.

The *Home Furnishings Daily* in the April 8, 1958, issue carried part of my speech in which I said that bright colored cars would not be in great abundance, that there would be fewer "two-tone" jobs and almost no "three-tones" will come off the production lines of 1959 and 1960. Neither will there be a general return to black; further, that in 1959 and 1960, cars will have very little chrome. These are the kind of changes that the automotive industry can make in the last phase of production and they will do so to meet public demand, a demand that was created primarily by the Sputniks and other events that shook our complacency.

Again, I make a prediction, on the basis of further studies conducted in 1958, that the jukebox effect will disappear from cars. Elaborate ornamentation of chrome and multiple colors will be minimized in 1960 cars, and purely decorative chrome will be discarded in 1961 cars. Car makers will make the changes because car buyers will not want to pay for the dazzle. The Sputniks caused an awareness of being ostentatious and impractical and have made consumers self-conscious and design-conscious.

Indirectly, the Sputniks and missiles had a greater effect on the American car market than any other single factor. The Russian satellites and the resulting publicity have made us feel frivolous and impractical. A Russian scientist said that the Russians were building satellites while we were concentrating on auto fins. This piece of news that was widely publicized struck us to the core. This marketing factor was, of course, not predictable.

As I have already pointed out, a major reason the Edsel has not been a success was not due primarily to the Sputniks. The basic reasons for marketing failure was the styling of the car not being based on research, on tests that reveal true attitudes, and the design lacking the image of modernity. The car was promoted as a new and revolutionary car. When it came out people thought it was an old-fashioned Mercury. There was a letdown. In addition, the change in the economic situation cut the sale not only of cars but also of other hard goods.

The Edsel management could have tested various car designs and designs of parts—grille, light assembly, bumpers, fenders etc.,—without revealing what the new car would be like. If they had done this, if the tests had been of the unconscious-level type (controlled motivation research) they would never have come out with this design.

In an association test we conducted with the Edsel car as soon as it was revealed, the respondents were asked to associate the car (photo) with one of five models—1935, 1940, 1945, 1950 and 1955. The car was associated with 1935 by the greatest number of respondents. Also, other negative associations were revealed in the test. When we tested the four-seater Thunderbird when it first came out, we found that it had a very high percentage in all favorable associations.

Recent studies also reveal that consumers are beginning to resent forced obsolescence. When yearly fashion changes were limited to women's apparel there was almost universal acceptance. The public did not resist the car design changes every year. Then other hard-goods makers began planned obsolescence. Perhaps this has broken the camel's back. Now the consumer is in revolt.

The 1958 studies showed that we should expect consumer resistance to elaborate ornamentation, non-functional gadgets, meaningless symbols and forced obsolescence, in all products. We have some evidence that it would be advisable for car makers to change the basic styling of their cars every three years, not every year, and the style changes should be coordinated with product improvement. There are many indications that the car with the greatest simplicity in design will be greatest in demand.

As for brand image, it will have to be backed up by product quality. Empty symbols will not be acceptable to the man in the age of rockets and satellites. Marketing men should not underrate the psychological effect, a sobering one, that the Sputniks, Atlas, the hydrogen bomb experiments and the intercontinental rockets have had on the American people.

Subliminal Projection

On September 19, 1957, I told the United Press that I considered subliminal projection in the same realm with flying saucers and prenatal regression under hypnosis. Not long before the interview with me, the daily papers and business press reported that a message saying "eat popcorn" and one saying "drink Coca-Cola" were flashed on the screen of a movie theatre for 1/3000 of a second at five second intervals. The patrons did not see the messages, but the commercials registered on their unconscious minds, according to these reports.

For many years, there have been experiments conducted in subliminal perception. Many psychologists have conducted tests in extrasensory perception. There is some evidence that extrasensory perception is possible under some circumstances.

I pointed out that at 1/3000 of a second there can be no image impression at all, conscious or unconscious. Besides, advertisers have a difficult enough job in creating motivating ads that are expected to reach consumers through their senses, visual and auditory. Out of every ten ads we test, we are fortunate if we find one or two that are effective with people who see them. I, for one, have been taking for granted that an ad is a complete failure if people don't see it.

I should mention, that later reports claimed that the images in subliminal projection were flashed at speeds of 1/50th of a second. (*Life*, March 31, 1958). This is no longer subliminal. During the war men could identify images of aircraft that were projected at 1/100th of a second.

I told the United Press reporter that most perception or most sensation remains unconscious. Our behavior is affected by unconscious or subliminal perception.

Although subliminal projection has been used experimentally in psychological laboratories it is of no practical significance.

For most of us mortals, before there is perception there has to be sensation, and in order to have sensation we must have sensory organs.

All animals do not have the same kind of sensory organs and all human beings do not have the same threshold of perception.

I know a man who has a whistle with which he calls his dog. The man cannot hear the whistle, but the dog can, because the dog has the organs that can receive the sound waves of the special kind of whistle.

Insects can see colors that human beings cannot see, because they have the organs for receiving the waves of light which make up those colors.

Subliminal perception and subliminal stimulation are always with us. The effectiveness of advertising is mostly subliminal. In other words, we are not always conscious of most of the ads and commercials, but unconsciously we are affected by them. Actually, any learning process is mostly subliminal.

However, we can be influenced either subliminally or consciously by ads and commercials. The promoters of subliminal projection claimed that the message can be received only subliminally, never consciously.

Another fallacy in subliminal projection is the assumption that people do what they are told, that if they are told to drink Coca-Cola, they will. We need not be concerned about this, since there cannot be any visual perception without visual sensation.

It is true that an image can be projected in such a way, that in an audience of several thousand there may be some few who have highly sensitive visual senses and would see, unconsciously or consciously, the message or image of which the great majority would be completely unaware. Obviously, it is not practical to have commercials for such a limited number.

I have read serious discussions about legislation for controlling the use of subliminal projection. If we were to have such legislation, I suggested we ask Congress at the same time to create government control agencies to regulate trips to Mars and to set up traffic rules for flying saucers.

The fact that subliminal projection was not anything to be taken seriously was predictable. Anyone who has gone deeply into the study of perception knows that perception begins with sensation. Therefore, where there was no sensation, there could be no perception. In 1957 there was no need to conduct tests in this field.

Don't Ask

People's behavior is not predictable by asking them what they will do or how they will act in relation to a product. They either don't know what they will do or they think they know but don't think they should tell you.

The following are examples of consumers not knowing the true answer:

In a test of three detergent packages, over 60 per cent of the women, after using the detergents from all three packages, were of the opinion that one of the packages contained a detergent that was strong and for heavy duty. Only 27 per cent thought that one of the other packages was for heavy duty. Only 13 per cent found the three detergents about the same. All three were actually the same. The packages caused most of the women to believe the contents were different.

Few individuals will tell you that they buy magazines because of the ads. They are not aware and they cannot tell you that ads have much psychological and social significance to them. Consciously, many people buy magazines for the editorial or literary content; unconsciously, they buy certain magazines because of the type of ads.

During World War II, a magazine was offered to a group of soldiers in two editions, the regular issue and a special overseas edition from which the ads were eliminated. Out of more than three hundred men, only twenty-two wanted the much smaller and lighter weight overseas edition without the ads, although the men were made aware that they were being shipped overseas and that the heavier magazine would be an added burden.

To ask people whether they value ads is meaningless and

wasteful effort. In direct interviews, individuals say that they are not interested in ads, but in their choice of magazines they show that ads are of interest to them.

A number of studies showed that individuals who claimed that they were not influenced by advertising, unconsciously bought only widely advertised products.

Their conscious minds rejected advertising, but their unconscious behavior showed that they were influenced by it, subliminally or unconsciously.

The following is a report of one of many studies showing that people cannot tell you what they have seen.

Men and women were given eye-movement tests on three pages of a newspaper.

After 24 hours the subjects were interviewed on what they had seen and read the previous day.

The following shows the verbalized responses and what they had actually seen as recorded by the eye-movement camera.

For areas seen (as revealed by the eye-movement camera), claims of having seen the areas were 68% for page 1, 62% for page 2 and 68% for page 3.

For areas partially seen (as revealed by the eye-movement camera), claims of having seen the areas were 60% for page 1, 47% for page 2 and 61% for page 3.

For areas not seen (as revealed by the eye-movement camera), claims of having seen the areas were 29% for page 1, 11% for page 2 and 26% for page 3.

This study shows that when people are asked to recall what they have seen, there is a considerable difference between what they say they saw and what they actually saw, as recorded by an instrument.

In another study with a large sample of consumers, the respondents were asked to indicate where they had seen each of twelve products advertised—television, newspaper or magazine.

Twenty-two per cent of the respondents said that they had seen

Hershey's Chocolate on television, 39% said they had seen it advertised in the newspapers and 52% said they had seen it advertised in magazines. This product has not been advertised in any of these media.

Dole Pineapple, Clapp's Baby Food, Cannon Towels, Cadillac Cars and Champion Spark Plugs have not had advertising time purchased for them on television (according to Standard Advertising Register). However, from 22% to 46% of the respondents reported that they had seen these products advertised on television.

This shows that a large percentage of individuals are not able to tell where they saw a product advertised. It also means that individuals often are not aware which advertising source motivated them to buy a product or how they were motivated.

The actual results of the study follow:

Identification of Product Advertising with Three Media

(Per Cent of Individuals)

Products	TV	Newspaper	Magazine
Hershey's Chocolate	22%	39%	52%
Dole Pineapple	33%	57%	68%
Clapp's Baby Foods	29%	44%	57%
Cannon Towels	22%	52%	72%
Cadillac Cars	44%	65%	78%
Champion Spark Plugs	46%	40%	65%
Adolph's Meat Tenderizer	15%	28%	32%
Life Savers	26%	41%	76%
Arrow Shirts	25%	54%	75%
Ocean Spray Cranberries	27%	52%	46%
Duncan Hines Cake Mixes	22%	28%	35%
Parliament Cigarettes	73%	53%	65%

We have much evidence that people remember little of what they see and generally are not aware whether they have or have not seen an ad. A proof of an unpublished ad was shown to women and they were asked, "Have you seen this ad before?" Sixteen per cent said they had. Yet they could not have seen it because it had never appeared in any publication.

A few weeks later the same persons were shown the same ad proof sheet and were asked the same question. Only twenty-two per cent of those who had seen the ad before, said they remembered it.

The proof sheet dealt with a cosmetic. The respondents were not trying to be misleading. They no doubt answered the question honestly, but their answers showed that most of them could not recall the ad.

We have just as much evidence that people cannot predict what they will do in the future. It was reported that Elmo Roper conducted a survey to forecast public response to *Life* magazine. The study showed that *Life* magazine would not be a success. We all know that there was something wrong with the prediction.

The national elections of 1948 were an outstanding example of the unreliability of polling methods. Dr. Gallup, Mr. Roper and other pollsters failed to predict the election results because many just didn't know or would not say how they would vote. People could tell the interviewer what they thought they would do when they walked into the voting booth, and sometimes they did. What people think they will do and what they actually do when they have to act are often entirely different.

Still another factor that weakens the structure of research based on polling methods is an unwillingness to give true information. To a pollster's question, "Have you borrowed money from a personal loan company?" a poll showed that no one had. But the loan company's records showed that all those interviewed had borrowed money.

Another well known example is a survey on what magazines people read. To the question, "What magazines do you read?" a poll indicated that the *Atlantic Monthly* had six times its actual circulation and that the pulp magazines, printed in the millions, had a negligible circulation. Obviously, many of those questioned were unwilling to go on record as lowbrow even though they enjoyed reading "lowbrow" publications.

We have conclusive evidence that research of the polling type, based on conscious reactions, is not a reliable tool because: 1) people do not have the ability to give the right information, 2) people are not always willing to give the right information.

Research that is conducted on an unconscious level with controlled tests is reliable. The validity of unconscious level testing has been established. It can be and is being used for predicting consumer behavior in the market place, because it reveals actual consumer reactions and attitudes which consumers either cannot talk about because they are not actually aware of them or do not want to reveal them because social status is involved.

Controlled research is no substitute for judgment and decision. Judgment enters into the research picture when a decision has to be made on what should or should not be tested. Judgment based on experience has to be used in designing the test for the particular problem. It is again needed in interpreting the research results and in making effective use of the findings.

As for "intuition and discipline," intuition has been replaced By the knowledge of how to reach the unconscious mind and research that is valid has the discipline. Research includes statistics which are elements of discipline. To be of value, the statistics must be of true attitudes of people, of their deep feelings and of their real motivations.

Studies show that consumers' motivations remain relatively the same for long periods of time. People's interests change very little under normal, social and economic conditions. A great social or economic change has a great effect on people's behavior and their wants.

The behavior of consumers cannot be predicted if a great social or economic change has taken place between the time of the study of consumer attitudes and the time of marketing. However, under normal social and economic conditions, consumers' behavior in relation to a product can definitely be predicted.

CHAPTER 6

DOGS, BUYERS AND SELLERS

MY BROTHER has a dog, a medium sized French poodle, who throws suspicion on the teachings of Sigmund Freud, the father of psychoanalysis. Freud disclosed that neurotic men and women got that way because they were not loved in their infancy and early childhood. I accepted Freud's conclusions that lack of love caused neurosis until I met Fifi. This dog, Fifi, not only had the love of her natural mother, but is equally loved by her foster mother. No baby can get more love than Fifi gets. Actually, Fifi gets the love of five mothers. The mama of the household fondles her, the papa fights for her affection, the older daughter caresses her, the younger daughter sleeps with her and the son romps with her. They all play with her and all feed her. Fifi is neurotic. She is spoiled, unmanageable, doesn't know what she wants or how to behave in the company of other dogs. She behaves almost as badly as some human beings.

Although Fifi in no way leads an ordinary dog's life, I often think, "Poor Fifi." She gets an overabundance of love, but she has nothing to say about the kind of food she eats. Her mama, that is her foster mother, buys her food. Although my sister-in-law has good taste in food as well as other kinds of good taste, she never actually tastes Fifi's food.

My sister-in-law is a very intelligent woman. She tells you, Fifi gets the best food there is. She was asked how she knows that Fifi gets the best food if she hasn't tasted it. "By the label, of course," she answered without hesitation. My sister-in-law and her intelligent husband find nothing wrong with this answer.

What would a foolish woman or an ignorant man say if he were asked how he knows that his dog gets the kind of food he should have? Without doubt, the answer would also be, "I can tell by the label whether the food is the kind that is fit for my dog."

There are no smart people or foolish people, when it comes to dogs and dog food. Most people who own dogs love them and almost none of them ever taste the food they give their dogs. They all know whether the food is fit for their dog by looking at the label of the can or box that contains the dog food.

Since the poor dogs, no matter how otherwise pampered, have nothing to say about what they eat, dog-food packers have to appeal to men and women who do the buying. They have to have packages that make dog owners believe that what is in the package is good for their dogs.

What kind of a package or label creates an impression of high quality, what kind of shape or dimension, what color, what type-style or lettering has the connotation of high quality?

When I was a little boy, if I wanted to know the answer to a question, I asked my mother, my father or my teacher and I usually was given the answer, the correct one, I thought.

But men and women don't get answers quite so easily from other men and women. Like Fifi, the French poodle, most people don't often know what they want or like, and frequently when they think they know, they don't want to tell you because they feel if they do reveal their feelings they might be put in a bad light.

In interviews, an individual generally likes to make a favorable impression on the interviewer. One respondent wants to let you know that he is modern, although actually he enjoys only old-fashioned things. Another wants to create the impression that he appreciates the cultural and historical value of antiques, whereas actually he can't stand having them around.

Studies that were conducted under controlled conditions show that men and women try to give rational answers in interviews, but their actions are emotional, not rational. In interviews, respondents seldom say that they like an object because of its styling, a package because of the design or an article because of the label. Motivation studies reveal that styling, packages, designs and labels cause people to buy, but the people won't tell you that they buy for these reasons.

Tests that were conducted on an unconscious level showed that consumers were motivated to buy a product because the package had an appealing crest. A new trademark increased the sale of a brand of sports clothes over 50%. A new sign doubled business for a retail store. We have dozens of examples of new packages increasing sales, and we have examples of new packages that were responsible for a great drop in sales.

In interviews, shoppers will normally not tell you that they buy a certain brand of food because they like the package. They will not tell you that they do not buy a certain brand because they do not like the package or label. The respondents generally like to talk about how good or how appetizing the product is. There is, however, at least one exception—dog food. When it comes to dog food, respondents don't talk about taste; they talk only about brand, which they know by the label.

When one wrapper that was created by a well-known designer was tested, the tests showed that if this new wrapper were used, it would lose about 60% of the current volume of sales. Tests of another wrapper showed that sales could be expected to increase about 35%, provided all other marketing factors remained about the same, that is, if social and economic conditions remained about the same, if the distribution facilities, promotion, advertising and price were not radically changed and if competition did not do something startling.

Testing is complex because people are not aware that they are influenced by symbols, by images of all kinds, (crowns, crests, ovals and circles) and by colors.

To measure display effectiveness with instruments is not difficult. To determine consumer attitudes and to predict consumer action require special methods and complex techniques that are borrowed from the field of psychology and psychoanalysis.

Deep in the subconscious in every one of us there is a battle raging constantly in our waking and sleeping hours. We have dreams at night and some of us have daydreams. All of us have conflicting emotions and conflicting drives. There is evidence that women have more inner conflicts than do men. Men are generally so busy with the outer battles that they don't have as much time for inner commotions.

Little things that are meaningless from a practical point of view may have great emotional meaning through their symbolism. Images and colors are often great motivating forces.

Some time ago we conducted a study of women shopping in an apparel shop. A young woman wanted to buy a blouse that was available in several colors. She held the blue blouse up to her face and looked into the mirror. She was a blonde and she knew she looked good in blue. She fingered the red one lovingly. She loved the color, she thought, but she said it was too strong and loud. The salesgirl reminded her that yellow was the fashionable color. She could not make up her mind between the color that she looked best in, the color she liked best and the color in current fashion, so she settled on a gray blouse. It was reported to me a couple of weeks later that she didn't like the gray blouse. "It was dead," she said. She wore it only twice.

Some of the other purchasers of blouses permitted one of the inner drives to win. Some bought blouses because the color flattered them; others chose the color that was in fashion and some took the color they liked. Each chose a color that satisfied the strongest urge or fulfilled the greatest wish. Just think! All this deep psychology in the mere process of buying a blouse.

About 400 women were asked which of two wrappers they liked better. Many of them said that the wrapper did not make any difference to them. Others said they liked the wrapper in six colors better than the one in three colors. But when the house-wives were asked to try the two products and to report which of the two they thought was of better quality, a large majority reported that the product in the three-color wrapper was the bet-ter of the two. When they were told that they could have a third package free, most of them wanted the product in the three-color package.

Actually, both packages contained exactly the same product. They transferred the sensation from the package to the product. Unconsciously, they felt that the three-color package was the finer of the two, so they assumed that the contents were of better quality. In the interview about the wrappers, most of them said they liked the six-color wrapper better, which they probably judged according to their art standards.

The reasons for the expression of preference for the six-color wrapper may not be important. We believe we know at least some of the reasons for the preference. What is very important is that in the interviews the respondents said one thing, but their behavior or action in relation to the product was the opposite. This episode demonstrates that management should not make decisions on the basis of what people say in answer to a direct question.

We can't ask housewives to eat the dog food in order to find out whether they transfer the sensation from the package to the product. In such a case, we conduct a visual test only, a controlled association test, designed to disclose the consumers' attitudes toward the package or product.

The following dog-food package study shows some of the problems that confront marketing research people.

First of all, the old label was put through ocular measure-ments—visibility, readability and eye-movement tests. These tests showed that the label should be improved in display effectiveness.

After the recommended changes were made, the label passed the ocular tests, which meant that the visibility of the package as a whole from the shelf, the readability of the brand name and the eye-flow and attention-holding were as they should be.

There now remained two psychological factors, appeal elements, to be solved. One was the type of dog that should be on the label and the other the background color.

Our records, of many studies with consumers on packaging food products, show that red is a more appropriate color for packages of meat products than blue. The tests of meat products, with large samplings of consumers, show that most reds have a direct association with "meat," whereas blue has no association with "meat" or with any other food. We, therefore, recommended that a red be used as a background for the new label instead of the blue of the old label.

Management and the advertising agency thought that the dog on the label should have a friendlier appearance, and they obtained art of another dog.

We at Color Research Institute designed a test that would reveal the attitudes of dog owners toward each of the dog pictures. The following are the test results.

Test No. 1 was of a new red label with a new dog illustration, against the same new label design with the old dog illustration. In this test the label with the new dog illustration had 61% favorable associations and the label with the old dog had 39% favorable associations. The test was conclusive. The new dog upgraded the brand. There was no question about that.

Test No. 2 was of the red label with the new dog illustration, that did well in test No. 1, against the old blue label. In this test, the red label with the new dog illustration had 63% favorable associations and the old blue label had 37% favorable associations. This test showed clearly that the new red label design with the new dog illustration is an effective marketing tool.

Tests No. 1 and No. 2 were conducted in areas where the brand was not known. Then came the question from management, "What about where the brand is known, how will the red label do there?"

We, therefore, tested the new red label with the new dog illustration against a blue label with the new dog illustration. The previous tests had already shown clearly that the new dog illustration was an asset. The question now was about the label background, whether it should have the red or the blue background.

The test results were as follows: In area No 1, the red label had 64% favorable associations. The blue label had 36%.

In area No. 2, the red label had 58% favorable associations. The blue label had 42%.

In area No. 3, the red label had 59% favorable associations. The blue label had 41%.

Examination of reports of studies of packages of five other brands of dog food confirmed that red was more effective than blue for dog food packages. In each case red had a high association with "meat" and with "high quality."

The three tests where this brand was well known confirmed the previous tests conducted in areas where the brand was not well known.

There was still another question from management. What are the attitudes of the old customers of this brand toward the red label?

Package designers generally want to make radical changes in packages and often management has reasons for making a radical change in a package or a line of packages. However, research has shown that a complete package change is not advisable for a well established brand unless the change is tied in with a big advertising campaign.

The best example of a coordinated package change and advertising program was Philip Morris cigarettes. "Pardon Us While We Change Our Dress" was featured in all the advertising media. The ad containing the old and the new packages plus an attractive young lady changing her dress had great impact and appeal.

In the case of this dog-food label, the basic design remained the same. Our laboratory tests—visibility, readability and eye-movement—showed that the new label was considerably more effective in display than the old one.

The dog illustration was new, but it was of the same breed of dog. Changing the color from blue to red would not change the identity of the label radically. Nevertheless, consumers often identify products by the dominant color of the label.

We had unquestionable evidence that red is a better color for a dog food than blue. Would the old buyers of the brand unconsciously or consciously have negative attitudes to the change of the color?

I have already told about the problems we have in testing because consumers don't know what affects them or what they want, and when they think they know they won't tell you. Another difficulty in marketing research is that the clients are also human. Company presidents and marketing managers have their personal likes and dislikes and they know not or care not why. They also have to contend with the personal opinions and various attitudes of their associates and assistants.

In the case of this dog-food label, we had a request from the client to conduct a store shelf test. One reason we don't consider store shelf tests reliable is that they are not controlled. Shelf position and location in the store are factors. The test results are black or white. Either one or the other moves off the shelf faster, but you don't know why. You still don't know whether the better of the two is as good as it could be; you don't know what particular element on the label motivates the shopper to take the package. Also, store tests are costly. Before you go to the expense of producing labels for an actual test market, you should know that you have an effective package. Besides, you reveal to competition that you are revising your marketing program.

However, in this case the packer already had both red and blue labels so that some of the objection to store-shelf testing was eliminated. Arrangements were made by our office to test in two stores.

The cans with red labels and those with blue labels were placed in equal stacks side by side for a period of four weeks. The positions of the red and the blue labels were reversed from left to right or vice versa on alternate weeks. One of our field men checked each store every day.

We should remember that the two labels were alike except for the background color. There was no reason given on the can or in any other way for the presence of cans of the same brand, but with two different background colors.

The result of this store test was that the blue label (the old color) outsold the red label (the new color with all the favorable test ratings) by a ratio of 5 to 4.

To management people, this meant that the blue label was a more effective marketing tool than the red label. To the research people, this meant that something was wrong with the test, that some bias was present. We were sure that something went wrong with the test because it contradicted the results of the five other tests that were conducted under controlled conditions. Both stores were watched carefully by our field men. Where was the bias? What happened?

We do not conduct interviews with consumers when we want to find out deep, unconscious motivations. But this time we decided we might discover what went wrong by conducting direct interviews with dog-food buyers in the two stores where the shelf tests were conducted.

The interviews brought out the following responses:

"The real _____ is in the blue can." "The blue one is the original _____." "The red is a cheaper kind." "The red can is like the _____ stuff."

"How do you know that the blue is the original, the real, the quality product?" our interviewer asked. Most of them said, "I know from experience," or "I just know." Some said, "I saw the blue can on the billboards." Here was the clue.

While the test was in progress, billboards featuring the blue label were on display. The advertising identified the blue label with the brand. Instead of the advertising supporting the new red label, it was supporting the old blue label.

The old customers knew the blue label and they were given no reason for the change to red. The billboards were also seen by those who had not bought the brand before, for their dogs. They too were impressed with the image of the brand having a blue label.

This case demonstrates that marketing is not a one-track operation. It shows the complexity of a marketing problem and reveals the intricacies of testing marketing media.

It supports the concept that a label is a symbol, that it is not an end in itself. People do not think that they buy labels or packages, they believe they buy products or brands that are identified by labels or packages.

Changing a label makes no sense to the average consumer unless the change symbolizes a change of product. If the shopper is not told that the change of label symbolizes an improvement in the product, he often believes that the change is for the worse. In this case, the shoppers were "told" by advertising that the blue label was the high quality product; they were told nothing about the red label. They, therefore, assumed that the red label represented an inferior product.

I hope the executives of the company that packs the brand of dog food have learned a lesson from this case. We certainly have learned a great lesson. We have learned that we must emphasize more and more to our clients the following:

That shoppers should be given a reason for a label change, that is, that a radical change in a label should be tied in with a change in product or an improvement in product.

That an advertising program should be coordinated with the obvious label change.

That a new label should not be tested in an area where there is advertising that does not show the new label.

Dogs must depend on their masters and mistresses for their food. Because the owners of the dogs are human, unlike dogs, they judge food and all other products by symbols and are motivated by images and by colors, by brand names and by labels.

In order to find out what kind of a label or package will motivate dog owners to buy a particular brand, we must conduct tests with controls. We must make sure that some factor outside of what is being tested does not influence the respondents.

CHAPTER 7

ADVERTISING OF THE FUTURE

I HAVE ALREADY reported that studies conducted by our Motivation Research Division revealed that consumers' attitudes toward many products had changed drastically in the fall of 1957. The studies showed that as recently as the first half of 1957, the majority of Americans reacted favorably to gaudy ornamentation, clashing color combinations and elaborate chrome trim on cars and other products.

Later studies revealed that people were reacting unfavorably to ostentatious ornamentation, frills and functionless objects. The studies revealed a basic psychological change in the American people which could not possibly have been caused by the mild recession in 1958. I attributed this drastic change primarily to the Russian Sputniks.

The mild economic recession contributed to making the American people economy conscious. But the Sputniks reached into the depths of the American character. They caused a great soul-searching and self-examination and gave us an inferiority complex. We became aware suddenly that, while we were occupied with useless gadgets and frills, the Russians were producing world-shaking objects. The Sputniks made us more serious and more discriminating.

Other studies conducted during 1958 revealed that the

LOUIS CHESKIN

American public is reacting negatively to certain types of advertising, particularly to certain kinds of television commercials.

A question often asked is why are national advertisers not using the screens in movie theatres for advertising their products? The answer recently given by a theatre man was that most commercials which appear on T.V. screens are not fit for theatre screens. "They irritate and antagonize the viewers and are, therefore, not acceptable to theatre operators."

In many communities, particularly in small towns with one or two theatres, filmed commercial messages are used to advertise the wares of local stores. Few large theatres in metropolitan centers have filmed commercials.

There is little prospect for the type of commercials that dominate the T.V. screens ever to reach the theatre screens in large cities where competition for customers is great. We have evidence that at home the viewer escapes the irritating commercials by going to the washroom or walking into the kitchen for a drink or a snack. These are not the kinds of escapes that people can have in the theatre.

Great advantages of theatre screen advertising are that the theatre screen commercials have a captive audience. However, people pay for theatre tickets to be entertained, not to be exposed to irritating commercials. Theatre operators say that they have enough problems attracting audiences without the handicap of irritating commercials. They are of the opinion that bad commercials would diminish the captive audience.

Many theatre operators are aware that commercials need not necessarily be irritating. They are aware of the profit potential. They show considerable interest in commercials that can be shown in theatres without antagonizing the audiences.

There are reports that over 200 national advertisers are already using theatre screens for advertising their products. More national advertisers will no doubt show an active interest in theatre screen advertising as soon as they find out that such advertising is available and profitable.

Recent studies of T.V. commercials conducted by our Motivation Research Division indicate that most of the commercials are not fit for the theatre screen. These studies confirm the opinions of theatre men.

There are commercials in existence that are fit for the theatre screen. The commercials I have in mind were, however, not produced in the greatest commercial country oft earth, the U.S.A. They were created in European countries where they are a major advertising medium. The European theatre commercials are from one to four minutes in length, whereas American commercials are of 40 to 90 seconds duration.

Among the best of the European theatre commercials are the award winning commercials of the 1956 Cannes Film Festival. I have seen the English, French, German and Italian award-winning commercials and have watched audience reactions to them. I saw that each of the prize winners delighted the audiences.

These European theatre commercials are varied in character. Some have puppets; some use ballet and classical music. Abstract designs and fantasy sketches are also employed for getting messages across to the audience.

Each is a work of art designed to entertain and get a message across at the same time.

These commercials were not created on the premise that for a commercial to be effective it merely must be remembered. They were obviously designed with the same objectives as any film show, to entertain. The success of the selling message depends primarily on the degree and kind of entertainment.

The enthusiastic reactions of American audiences to the Cannes Festival commercials prompted at least one research man to want to find out whether the commercial message was remembered. A recall test with a small sampling of viewers revealed that each of the commercials had a high degree of recall. What is much more significant is that each of the commercials left a clear image in the mind of the viewer, an image with favorable associations and meaningful connotations which were directly related to the selling message. These commercials had great impact and at the same time had a deep, psychologically favorable effect on the audience in spite of the limitations of a foreign language.

Most American advertising specialists depend primarily on copy for getting their messages across. Language is their basic means of communication. American commercials consist largely of slogans, rhyming lines or dramatic declarations. The Europeans make appeals to the senses with significant images, stimulating colors, inspiring music, dramatic movement and meaningful symbols.

The prime objective of the European producers was to entertain, to amuse, to please. The selling is indirect, subtle, unobtrusive, not overbearing as most American commercials are.

These commercials do not bring out defense mechanisms in the audience. The viewers do not react to them any differently than they do to the main feature in the theatre. Psychologically, the European theatre commercials are akin to the shorts, comedies, cartoons and travelogs used in American theatres.

One of the main reasons that we are not producing commercials like the Europeans is that American advertisers generally insist on having the obvious. They demand "hard sell." They want to hit the audience hard and fast. Recent tests conducted on an unconscious level disclose that the hard-hitting, fleeting commercials irritate and antagonize more consumers than they attract.

The recent studies of a number of representative commercials show clearly that most of them do not motivate consumers to buy. They merely succeed in making the consumer aware that the products exist or are available. Consumers often buy the product in spite of, not because of, the character of the commercial.

The studies show that the more aggressive the commercial is in its selling aspect, the less it sells; the less obvious the selling purpose, the more effective is the commercial. The "soft sell" is more effective than the "hard sell." The "soft sell" or "indirect selling" puts the emphasis on the buying, on motivating people to buy.

The direct commercial puts the emphasis on selling and makes the consumer feel that he is being high-pressured. Many are antagonized by the same old sales pitch. This fact is still difficult for most American advertisers to accept.

Martin Mayer has in his book, *Madison Avenue, U.S.A.* (Harper & Brothers, 1958), the following:

> Around our shop we like to use parables, and Bill Kearns, our president, tells one about a farmer who all his life wanted to buy a superior mule. He saved his money, and paid two thousand dollars for a mule, they tell me that's a good price for a mule, but he got a stubborn one. When he got it into the barn it wouldn't move. So he chained it to the tractor and dragged it ten miles down the road to a mule trainer.
>
> The mule trainer said he would train the mule, and the farmer asked him how much. 'Five dollars,' said the mule trainer.
>
> 'That's a reasonable price,' said the farmer. 'Go ahead.'
>
> The mule trainer dragged the mule into his barn, picked up a forty-five-pound sledgehammer and hit the mule right between the eyes. The mule went off like this.
>
> 'For God's sake,' cried the farmer, 'I hired you to train him, not to kill him!'
>
> 'Sure I'll train him, but first,' said the mule trainer, 'first I've got to get his attention.'
>
> —Rosser Reeves,
> chairman of the board Ted Bates & Company

> Every advertisement must be considered as a contribution to the complex symbol which is the brand image. . . . I am astonished to find how many manufacturers, even among the new generation, believe that women can be persuaded by logic and argument to buy one brand in preference to

another—even when the two brands are technically identical. . . .

The manufacturers who dedicate their advertising to building the most favorable image, the most sharply defined personality for their brands are the ones who will get the largest share of these markets at the highest profit—in the long run."

—Speech by David Ogilvy

I dreamed I was Cleopatra in my Maidenform Bra
        —Advertisement by Norman, Craig & Kummel

The Rosser Reeves story expresses an advertising philosophy that is still dominant in the advertising field. "Hard sell" is what it is called. Its basic principle is to hit the consumer hard and frequently, psychologically, as hard as the mule trainer hit the mule. I am sure this method worked in the days when there were more customers than products, when people wanted the product so badly they were willing to be insulted and irritated. But a few things have happened recently. People can no longer be motivated to buy products by being treated like mules.

David Ogilvy represents a completely different and new philosophy of advertising. He is a highly intelligent and well-informed man, and he is fully aware of what has been going on in the field of psychology. To him, human beings are not purely biological, they are not mules. Nor are they rational or logical.

Basically, David Ogilvy builds all his advertising copy on "prestige identification." He is essentially an image builder, a personality maker. His advertising gives the product a distinct character and a specific and interesting personality. David Ogilvy sells "status."

To my knowledge, no one has studied the role of the corporate image more than Pierre Martineau of the *Chicago Tribune*, author of *Motivation in Advertising* (McGraw-Hill, 1957). Says he:

If a company or a brand is saddled with a negative image, even the most realistic and functional qualities of its products will be colored and altered. We find reasons to reject what we do not like. And at the other extreme, when the feeling tone is favorable to the corporate image, we persistently look for the good side of every experience with this company and its products. This is why any consideration of corporate images has to be concerned with feeling tone and emotive components as well as with the functional and intellectual meanings.

The extreme difficulty of changing a negative image stems from the fact that the individual's attitudes are embedded in a subrational matrix of feeling. He remains immune to logic. In our *Chicago Tribune* studies of nonconsumers in the newspaper field, these groups remained stubbornly oblivious to any changes or improvements in the newspapers they did not like. They will go on for years parroting the same attitudes which long since have ceased to have any basis in fact at all. For example, a newspaper, which had changed its name 13 years ago and had been sold in the meantime, was still associated with the same name and the same ownership as far as these nonconsumers were concerned. Their feelings simply would not let them accept reality.

I cannot help pointing out that the 1958 Edsel car and the 1958 Thunderbird are outstanding examples of two philosophies of marketing. The Edsel was used as a sledge hammer hitting the public over the head, hard and without let-up. The four-seater Thunderbird was a well engineered car, a beautifully designed vehicle and it was introduced to the public with dignity, self-confidence and pride. The ads featured the convenience aspects and beauty elements of the car. The advertising budget was relatively small.

Because people are not mules, they bought the Thunderbird but refused to buy the Edsel.

What makes the two car brands such good examples is that the new four-seater Thunderbird and the new Edsel were both introduced in 1958 and both are made by the same company. The basic philosophy of marketing the four-seater Thunderbird was totally different from that of the new Edsel. The Thunderbird was designed with an image of quality. The 1958 Edsel was merely advertised and promoted as an image of quality.

The objective of marketing is to get customers, which is not the same as making sales. Some advertising campaigns are effective in making sales but they can't get customers because the advertising can make only the first sale. The product itself has to help make the second sale. Many advertising campaigns have failed because of an inferior or unappealing product.

There is a story about an excellent marketing program on dog food that failed. The advertising was effective, the package was attractive and the price was competitive, but the dogs did not want to eat the food. Since there was no one else in the households of America that would eat that brand of food, the first purchase is all there was and the marketing program collapsed.

"I dreamed I was Cleopatra in my Maidenform Bra" and "I dreamed I went walking in my Maidenform Bra" are of course psychological themes strictly of the Freudian school. These are the kinds of ads that are found wanting when tested on a conscious level. Consciously, the ladies find the ads objectionable. Unconsciously, many are motivated to buy Maidenform brassieres.

Advertising men often talk as if they consider the coverage and saturation of advertising as the only factors in marketing. They frequently forget about the quality of the advertising. They sometimes consider advertising as if it were a static, distinctly formed entity.

Research that is conducted on an unconscious level and probes into the true motivations of potential consumers provides a basis for dividing advertising into three classifications. Of course, there are printed ads and filmed commercials with various degrees of effectiveness within each classification.

A: *Printed ads and filmed commercials that are informative, but neither motivating nor irritating.* They merely show and describe the product. The degree of success of such ads and commercials depends almost entirely on the coverage and saturation. The more people the communication reaches and the oftener the people are exposed to it, the greater will be the number of buyers of the product. We have found that the greatest percentage of printed advertising is in this classification.

B: *Printed ads and filmed commercials that are irritating.* The wider the coverage and the greater the saturation such printed ads and filmed commercials have, the bigger will the marketing failure be. The more people such printed ads and filmed commercials reach, the oftener the people are exposed to them, the fewer buyers of the product there will be.

C: *Printed ads and filmed commercials that are motivating, the kind of advertising that does not merely tell people to buy, but makes them want to buy.* Such advertising needs as much coverage, but not as much saturation as classification A advertising. An ad or filmed commercial that is motivating will be effective on first contact with the potential consumer, but the advertising, of course, has to reach the consumer at least once.

To those in the advertising and marketing fraternities who say that they have known irritating printed ads and irritating filmed commercials that have brought marketing successes, the answer is that those ads and commercials they have in mind were irritating to them. They were not irritating to the potential consumers.

Often, I find myself in a similar position. Marketing themes, ads, filmed commercials, brand-identifying images and packages that I personally think are bad turn out favorably in our tests. Many a marketing tool that I thought was good failed in the tests.

I don't think that I am an average consumer. I believe that reliance on my personal judgment is dangerous. The fact that I like a product, a design or a piece of copy very much should immediately put it under suspicion and classify it under the questionable-value list. I simply am not a typical consumer and do not believe that I can possibly react like one to anything. Experience has confirmed this.

We can now hope to have non-irritating commercials on T.V. and the kind that will be acceptable to theatre operators. We can anticipate such development in the advertising field because unconscious-level tests can be conducted to ascertain whether the public will react favorably toward the commercial and whether it will be effective in producing sales.

After more than a dozen years of experience with unconscious level tests for measuring the effectiveness of marketing media, some advertisers are aware that controlled motivation research techniques are reliable means for predetermining the effectiveness of filmed commercials and printed ads. More and more, advertisers are becoming aware of the role that unconscious level testing can play in marketing. More and more, advertisers are beginning to see the validity of this type of motivation research.

Another factor that will aid in developing the "indirect selling," entertaining type of commercial is the growing awareness that most of the effectiveness of a commercial is subliminal, that is, its effect is on the unconscious mind. All of us are influenced by advertising without being aware of it. People are motivated by a printed ad or T.V. commercial to buy a certain product, but often are not aware that they have been motivated by the particular ad or commercial. Generally, they are not conscious that they have been motivated by any advertising. They merely go to the store and buy the product without any thought about what motivated them.

The following is an excellent example of the subliminal effect of advertising. A man walked into a men's wear shop and asked for a Knox hat. The salesman said that they carried Stetson hats which are the same as Knox. The man insisted on having a Knox and went to three stores before he found a Knox hat. Why did he insist on having a Knox? When the question was put to him, he said he did not know exactly why. He thought that Knox hats were the best. When it was pointed out to him that his old hat was a Mallory, he said he had recently found out that the Knox people made a better quality hat. He could not remember where the information came from.

The man invited me to his home for dinner. On the way to his house in his car, I saw a billboard advertising Knox hats. I learned that the billboard had been there for over two months and it was plainly visible from an intersection with stop-and-go lights. Obviously this billboard motivated the man to want a Knox hat.

This subliminal or subconscious effect should not be confused with the publicity given subliminal projection in 1957. Subliminal projection is more in the realm of the occult than the scientific. It should not be confused with the effect of all good advertising on an unconscious level. An effective ad, poster, T.V. or theatre commercial is effective on a conscious and on an unconscious level. Any ad that affects the unconscious mind can also affect the conscious mind. Sometimes an individual is aware that he is being influenced by an ad and at other times he does not know that his desire to buy an article had been brought about by an ad.

Psychologically speaking, there is no perception without sensation, and perception can be either conscious or unconscious, that is, the effect can be below the threshold of consciousness, or subliminal. The exponents of subliminal projection claimed that the messages could be received only subliminally; the viewers could not see the commercials if they wanted to.

I have already covered this subject and touch on subliminal projection here merely to make sure that there is no confusion between subliminal projection and the subliminal effect of all good advertising matter.

Advertisers who are aware that advertising is largely effective subliminally will have no difficulty in accepting the principle that advertising can be tested, and should be, on an unconscious level, that is, tested without the respondents being aware that the ad or commercial is being tested.

Conversely, advertisers who are aware of the successful testing of ads on an unconscious level will have no difficulty accepting the fact that ads are effective on an unconscious level, that people are not always aware they are being influenced by ads or filmed commercials.

Those who insist on commercials being literal want marketing tests to be literal. Those who only understand marketing tests that are direct interviews (polling and playbacks) will demand commercials that are direct, boring and irritating, thus minimizing the effectiveness of the advertising.

Such commercials will never reach the theatre screen because theatre operators do not have suicidal tendencies. Thus a most effective advertising medium is neglected and denied to national advertisers.

Our studies reveal that the effectiveness of "hard sell" is on the way out. It is going the way of gaudy ornamentation, loud uncomplementary and unrelated colors and a dominance of chrome on cars.

Immediately after the Second World War, there was a hunger for new products and there were consumers with more money than they knew what to do with. "Hard sell" commercials told the people where and how they could spend their money.

The great hunger for new products has subsided. Telling people about a new product is no longer enough. Consumers must now be motivated to buy.

Many consumers cannot be motivated to buy when they are antagonized or put on the defensive. Our studies show that there are now many more consumers who are repulsed by aggressive commercials than there were a year or two years ago.

The studies clearly show that consumers are irritated by the so-called "hard sell" commercials. The harder the sell, the less it motivates people to buy. But the "hard sell" commercials are easily recalled. The unpleasant sensation is remembered by many for a long time.

I have breakfast with Dave Garroway every weekday morning, although I am in Chicago and he is in New York. On one of his shows there was a demonstration of an interesting toy called a Hula Hoop. On another show he demonstrated a new product called "Velcro."

He explained that the name "Velcro" was formed out of the first syllables of velvet and crochet. This explanation provided an association that served as an aid in recalling the brand name. He showed how the product is used in garments. He told where the idea for the new product came from, and pointed out that tiny hooks and loops make the product work as it does.

The demonstration was natural, mild, unaggressive. It was integrated with the show. It was an attention-holding performance. It aroused a great interest in "Velcro." And the other show on which Hula Hoops were demonstrated sold many thousands of Hula Hoops.

Why did the Garroway show demonstrations make consumers buy Hula Hoops? Why were consumers motivated to want "Velcro?" The answer is simple. The demonstrations were natural. They appealed to basic human interests. They were an integrated part of the show. They did not antagonize. They did not put the audience on the defensive.

Dave Garroway's demonstrations and his commercials are friendly, not aggressive. They are mild, not strong. They are soothing, not irritating. They are soft, not hard. They attract, they do not repel. They do not merely tell people to buy the product, they motivate them to buy it.

I had the opportunity to watch Dave Garroway at close range in September of 1957 when I was a guest on his show on publication day of my book, *How to Predict What People Will Buy*. I learned much that morning merely by watching the operation of the show. I saw indirect selling, the "soft sell" in action.

Ed Sullivan is another master of the "soft sell." The manner in which he sells the Mercury and Edsel is not offensive to anyone.

The Prudential Insurance Company had a commercial that is an excellent example of "soft sell." It consisted of a couple discussing Prudential Insurance in the kitchen. It was a natural, soft presentation of a probable situation.

The Westinghouse sponsored "Desi and Lucy Fiesta" show that was on the television screens October 6, 1958, is an example of the kind of commercials that will dominate the screens in the near future. The commercial message was integrated with the show. It held interest because it was amusing instead of irritating. This commercial message is recalled as a pleasant experience, not an annoying one. If it is not consciously recalled, deep in the subconscious it rests in association with other pleasant experiences. It will become active and motivating when the kind of product made by Westinghouse is needed.

A basic error is in the assumption that emphasis on selling is the same as emphasis on buying. Our studies show clearly that the strongest selling does not mean the greatest buying.

We have conclusive evidence that printed ads or filmed commercials that are chosen on the basis of "playbacks" do not result in advertising of maximum effectiveness.

The belief that because an ad or a filmed commercial is easily recalled, it is therefore an effective marketing tool, is the weakest link in any present-day marketing situation.

There are many reasons why playbacks are still used for testing ads and filmed commercials. The most outstanding is the failure to recognize the subconscious or subliminal power of advertising.

Our studies disclose that the subconscious or subliminal effect of a good, pleasing, motivating ad or filmed commercial is much greater than the conscious or literal effect. Obviously, if one is not conscious of having seen an ad or commercial he cannot tell about it in an interview.

As far back as September, 1948, in the *Harvard Business Review*, I described tests demonstrating that people could not recall ads and objects to which they had been exposed unless they were motivated to do so. One example: Women did not remember seeing scissors in a room when they were asked what they had seen, but they recalled seeing the scissors when they needed a pair of scissors.

If playbacks are not reliable for measuring the effectiveness of advertising, how do we determine whether an ad is an effective selling tool? Where does "hard sell" begin or where does "soft sell" end?

We measure ad effectiveness by means of a series of tests, each of which reveals one aspect of effectiveness. Ads are first submitted to eye-movement tests, which show how the eyes flow over the ad, where they rest and how long they remain at each point. If the ocular test is favorable, if the ad has smooth eye-flow and attention is held at all vital points, it goes into field tests. The field tests are controlled association-type tests that reveal consumer attitudes and indirect preference tests that show consumer action or preference, in which self-interest is involved.

An important aspect of the testing procedure is the following: When we field-test ads, in one of the tests we do not actually test the ad. We test the product or the package by means of a controlled association and an indirect preference test. Then we test the product or package again in the same way, but in the presence of the ad, with a matched sample of consumers. The object is to see whether the ad upgrades or downgrades the product or brand without the respondents being aware that we are interested in the ad. This is what we mean by testing on an unconscious level. This is one type of unconscious-level test that is conducted by Color Research Institute.

Filmed commercials are tested in a similar manner. Controlled association-type tests are used for measuring the effectiveness of the commercial, and the product is tested before and after the subjects have been exposed to the commercial. The tests show whether the commercial upgrades or downgrades the product.

Most creative people resent research. Many copy writers and art directors consider research limiting and even stifling. Their attitudes are to a considerable degree justified. Direct testing methods, interviews, polls and playbacks do not reveal the effectiveness of copy or art that is subtle, that reaches the subconscious mind or that motivates people without their being aware that they are being motivated.

Quantitative research means counting heads, not souls, not feelings, not emotions, not inner meanings and not motivations.

Even research that is qualitative cannot always be reliable, if it is unstructured, lacks controls, consists of very small consumer samplings and depends on the particular skill of the researcher.

There is much evidence that many creative people in the advertising field have not yet had their greatest opportunities to demonstrate their talents and skills. They have been hampered by research that measures the effectiveness of advertising, only on a conscious level.

The advertising profession has not yet had its greatest opportunity in motivating people to buy and consume the products that our industry is capable of producing.

Management's insistence on having the obvious in advertising, with research measuring only the conscious effectiveness of the printed ad or filmed commercial, results in advertising that lacks maximum effectiveness.

However, there really is hope that the unconscious mind of the consumer will be taken into consideration by manufacturers of consumer goods. Business conditions are forcing management to look for new avenues. Many are opening their eyes and their minds.

Leading research people already recognize the unconscious

effect of advertising. Howard D. Hadley, Vice President in charge of research of the Bureau of Advertising of the American Newspaper Publishers Association, recognizes the importance of advertising effectiveness on an unconscious level. He knows that ads must not merely be remembered, but must motivate consumers.

More than ten years ago, I found that Joan A. Geiger of Ted Bates understood the need of testing marketing tools on an unconscious level. Perhaps Rosser Reeves, chairman of the board of Ted Bates & Company, is aware that people are not always conscious of their motivations.

More than six years ago I discussed unconscious-level testing with Larry Deckinger. He knew the value of measuring consumers' motivations, not their verbalisms. He showed an understanding of the techniques of testing on an unconscious level.

Dietrich Leonhard of George Fry & Associates knows the importance of testing motivations, not merely retention. He knows that determining attitudes is not the same as recording verbalisms. Leonhard and I first discussed motivation research as far back as 1946 or 1947.

This is the time for leaders in advertising to give full recognition to the unconscious or subliminal aspect of advertising. Now is the time for advertising to begin to stress buying, not selling. Much more consumer goods will be moved by printed ads and filmed commercials that do not merely tell people to buy, but motivate them to buy.

CHAPTER 8

WHAT KIND OF RESEARCH?

THE SERVICES of A. C. Nielsen Company, with headquarters in Chicago, are well known and widely used. When the Food-Drug Index was introduced by Nielsen, it was a revolutionary contribution to marketing, a major step in the direction of scientific marketing. For the first time, a manufacturer could have a clear picture of his share of the market. The reports coming every two months enabled the manufacturer to see whether he was gaining or whether competition was gaining. Comparing his results with that of competition enabled him to make marketing plans and to revise strategy.

Starch reports are probably the most widely used for measuring the readership of print advertising. The basic principle of Starch readership measurement is based on recognition. David Starch began his service thirty-five years ago. His "readership measurements" are based on the idea that the presence of an ad in a publication does not mean that the readers of the publication have seen it, that an ad can be effective only if people have seen it. His "measurements" are made on the premise that people will remember and tell you whether they have or have not seen an ad when it is shown to them or brought to their attention. In the interview, the respondent is asked whether he or she recognizes the ad. Many advertisers assume that ads with high "readership" are effective selling ads, that if an individual sees an ad he is automatically motivated to buy the product in the ad.

Gallup and Robinson "Impact" reports are as widely used as Starch "readership" reports, according to some specialists in the advertising field. The "Impact" measurements are based on the principle of "recall." Gallup and Robinson interviewers probe further than the Starch interviewers do. The respondent is asked to describe the ad, tell what the ad contained, what it said, what the respondent thought when he saw the ad and what kind of impression the ad made on him and how favorable or unfavorable it was. The interviewer writes down everything the respondent says.

Gallup and Robinson interviewers do not show the ads to the respondents until the major questions have been answered. Many respondents play back the ad without knowing what was advertised in it. Some of the things people say they thought about have nothing at all to do with the product.

Interviews are conducted on competitors' ads also. These interviews show whether the client's or the competitive sales appeals are having the greatest impact on potential consumers.

Television commercials are tested by Gallup and Robinson on the same basic principles. However, a verbatim transcription of a respondent's comments about television commercials is difficult to make, since the interviewer does not have the commercial for checking what the respondent is saying. This problem has recently been solved by recording what the respondent is saying. The interviewer carries a concealed battery operated tape recorder with him. The interview comes into the office in the original respondent's speech. Secretaries transcribe it into a typescript. The interviews, exactly as they were, plus analyses and recommendations, are sent to the client.

In addition to Gallup and Robinson and the Institute of Public Opinion, Gallup operates Audience Research, Inc. which measures the potential popularity of movies and television programs that have not yet been shown to the public.

An electronic device is used. Each member of the audience who is invited to the theatre has a dial to turn indicating the degree of pleasure or displeasure at each moment of the program. Electrical impulses from each of the dials make a continuous graph of total audience pleasure or displeasure.

After the show, the members of the audience have a discussion which is recorded and then analyzed.

One of the significant elements of this measurement of reactions to the films shown, in this special theatre with a special audience, is the fact that the graph shows great displeasure or irritation each time a commercial appears.

Interviewers contact members of the Research Theatre audience on the following day and put them through the regular type of Gallup and Robinson interview.

Schwerin Research Corporation also uses theatre audiences for measuring "the selling power" of television commercials. He uses a simulated sales situation to show how people change brand preferences because of advertising influence. He offers product gifts. The members of the audience have a choice of brands. When choosing a brand as a gift, the consumer or member of the audience is forced to make a decision similar to a decision she has to make when shopping.

After the members of the audience have chosen their gifts they are exposed to a television commercial and then are again asked to choose a gift. A comparison is made between the gifts that were chosen before the commercial was shown and the gifts that were chosen after the commercial was shown. The difference shows the power of the commercial. If the commercial causes a large percentage of the audience to choose the advertised brand as the second gift, the commercial is considered to be an effective one.

Spectators are asked to mark in a booklet they are given, spaces indicating liking, neutrality and disliking. After the show, which is of about half hour duration, with three one minute commercials, the spectators are asked to recall each of the commercials. They are asked to put down the brand name and anything else they can remember. The main purpose for this is to make the audience conscious of the commercials. Then the second prize is chosen. Later the members of the audience discuss the program and the commercials.

Some commercials make some members of the audience change their brand preferences after seeing the commercial in Schwerin's theatre. Other commercials do not produce any change at all. The percentage of shift in choice of brand depends on the type of product as well as on the effectiveness of the commercial and on the kind of entertainment program. Usually the shift is from 5% to 10%.

Nielsen National Television Index is reported to be the most widely used service for measuring the popularity of television programs. An electronic measurement device is used. It is a metal box called an Audimeter, the size of a small radio. It is attached to the TV set and it registers the hour and minute at which the set is turned on, the channel and length of time the set remains on each channel. According to reliable reports, there are almost 1,000 homes in the country equipped with Audimeters.

Trendex is another service for measuring the popularity of network programs. This service is based on telephone interviews. Names are chosen from the telephone book and those who answer the telephone are asked what television program they were watching at the time the telephone rang. This is a quick and inexpensive service. A Nielsen report takes from three to four weeks to get. A Trendex report is available on the following day.

There are dozens of organizations providing services in measuring the effectiveness of ads and filmed commercials. Starch, Gallup and Robinson, Schwerin and Trendex represent specific concepts of measurement. There are many using the techniques that were developed by Starch, and Gallup and Robinson, with headquarters in New York, and there are researchers who use other methods. Some maintain consumer panels for judging new products or product changes.

All of these research organizations, the pioneers and the imitators, have one thing in common. They all operate on the premise that advertising is effective only on a conscious level and that consumer buying is based on product familiarity. In other words, the assumption is that if the people see the ad they will buy the product it advertises. If people know about the product, they will want it.

The great progress that has been made in the behavioral sciences in recent years is given no recognition. The findings of psychoanalysis are given no attention. The unconscious mind is given no consideration. Subconscious motivations are not measured.

Defense mechanisms of respondents are not guarded against. Prestige identification factors and ego-involvements in interviews are not isolated. Interviewer bias is given no attention. Mostly verbalisms are measured, not motivations.

The most publicized man in the advertising and marketing fields who puts emphasis on consumers' motivations is Ernest Dichter, Director of the Institute for Motivational Research, whose activities are centered in New York City. The Institute "conducts research" in almost every marketing phase—marketing themes, ads, filmed commercials.

The Institute of Motivational Research makes use of general discussions with groups of consumers. Sampling procedures are completely disregarded. Social strata, economic status, educational background, etc., are not considered important marketing factors by Ernest Dichter and are given no consideration in his studies. Projective tests and depth interviews are used and Freudian theory is considered basic in almost all consumers' motivations.

Ernest Dichter himself and members of his staff put emphasis on their interpretation of the responses of subjects. They are interested in what people mean, not in what they say.

One advertising agency executive told me that he considered

Dr. Dichter the best copywriter he has ever known, but did not consider him a researcher.

Dichter says of himself that he is consumer-oriented, that is, he sees a product as the consumer sees it.

According to some, Dichter sees "Freudian" symbolism and nothing else in every product and he believes that every consumer is always interested in "Freudian" symbolism.

I believe that Dichter is a very competent psychologist and an astute analyst. He is also no doubt an idea man. He is a creative person. To me it seems paradoxical that he is identified with research. The depth interviewing techniques he uses are straight out of clinical psychology. These methods depend on skills. Controls cannot be used. Dichter does not produce statistics.

Dichter does not employ measurement instruments. He knows what generally motivates people, but he uses judgment, not measurement. He knows the importance of the unconscious mind. He recognizes that effective ads and effective filmed commercials are those that are motivating, not those that can merely be easily recalled.

How about members of the staff of the Institute of Motivational Research? Is it possible that they are as skillful in getting information from representative consumers, even when they are representative, as he is? If each of them is as skillful or nearly as skillful as Ernest Dichter, which is not likely, is it possible that they all interpret in the same way what the subjects say?

Undoubtedly, the Institute of Motivational Research operates on a sound psychological foundation. But where is the structure? Where are the supports for the ceiling? What is used as a means for detecting and eliminating bias? What standards are there? What check points are used? How is objectivity maintained? What evidence is provided that the conclusion is right?

Social Research, in Chicago, is also interested in motivations and it conducts both marketing and personnel studies. Burleigh Gardner, the director, and his staff have a reputation for being competent and reliable. They conduct projective tests and depth interviews mostly. They make considerable use of sentence completion tests. At Color Research Institute we found that such tests reveal more about the individual respondent than about the stimulus (trademark, package or ad). A sentence completion test is an excellent device for personnel testing, but not for discovering consumer attitudes toward a marketing tool. At Social Research emphasis is put on the consumer as a member of a social group. Therefore, sampling is given careful attention. However, to my knowledge, Social Research does not conduct controlled tests for measuring the effectiveness of marketing tools.

Ernest Dichter who comes out of Vienna, the cradle of psychoanalysis, apparently looks for Freudian symbolism in every product and libidinous meanings in every human action. Nearly every utterance attributed to him that has come to my attention indicates an almost complete preoccupation with Freudian symbolism and libidinous connotations. Ernest Dichter can be considered the "total psychoanalyst" of marketing.

Burleigh Gardner is the "total sociologist." He considers the consumer a social being, not a pleasure-loving individualist. Says Gardner:

"The individual is important, but so is the group which dictates much individual behavior. It is here that sociological and anthropological knowledge enter strongly into the motivation researcher's work. The motivation researcher must understand group behavior and apply this understanding to the particular problem which he is studying. The client must communicate with the individual, but he must also communicate effectively with the individual's group. Thus, both must be understood. Though Americans like to think of themselves as rugged individualists, it is the rare person who is willing to flout the feelings of his fellow men—to ignore the fact that the people around him are always sitting in judgment on what he says and does.

"The expert motivation researcher brings these two basic

premises together in each study. Through this combination—a study of the group relative to the particular product area—he is able to provide the X-ray of the market for his client.

"Depending on the problem at hand, motivation research can be expected to do several things.

1. It can give an understanding of the forces which are acting upon and motivating people. This may be a matter of 'principles,' if you will—principles which once understood can be applied to future problems as well as the immediate ones.
2. It can give a range of fresh ideas about a problem—ideas which may lead to improved approaches. This can be especially true in studying advertising and its communication.
3. It can provide specific answers to a variety of problems. It can indicate 'whys' and 'wherefores' and suggests guidelines for future actions."

Burleigh Gardner says the individual is important, but that the group dictates much individual behavior. A psychoanalyst, or motivation researcher Ernest Dichter, would say the individual is all or most important, that deep-seated attitudes are not changed by the social group.

Psychoanalysis has shown that emotional instability, unconscious repressions, sublimation, fixation, inhibition, regression, dependence, feeling of insecurity, all sorts of complexes, fetishes and phobias all originate in early childhood. Freud revealed that a person's cravings and actions are basically determined by natural needs and impulses and they are controlled and inhibited by social pressures. Freud pointed out that the individual can feel free to act only after he understands both his impulses and his inhibitions.

There is unquestionable evidence that strong likes and deep dislikes for objects have their beginnings in the very early stages of life. They are not the result of adult social experience or of group identification.

Objective examination of the two points of view, social and psychoanalytic, discloses that there is actually no conflict between psychoanalysis and sociology. The disagreement is between psychoanalysts and sociologists. Each of the sciences covers an aspect of human life and behavior. The human being is complex. He is biological, psychological and sociological in nature. A biologist (such as Kinsey) sees man in one way, a psychoanalyst looks at man in another light and a sociologist observes him in still another. But the human being plays all three roles— biological, psychological and social.

A "successful" man I know bought a Cadillac convertible car. He bought this brand of car because it is associated with social status, because it has prestige identification. He wanted a convertible because it is symbolic of youth and vigor with the unconscious, if not conscious, hope that it will suggest that he has youth and vigor. He chose a baby blue color because he loves baby blue; he does not know why, but there are deep unconscious reasons for this choice. Obviously, this man bought the particular car, not only for group identification, and not only for libidinous reasons.

When a woman buys a dress because it is in the latest fashion, she is expressing a wish to belong to "the group." It means she craves social status. When she chooses a garment that clings to her body and reveals "the best parts" of her figure, she is not being motivated by social considerations or group identification. If she chooses a color that she loves, but does not know why, she is acting as an individual, as a unique and distinctive character, independent of group identification.

Together, Ernest Dichter and Burleigh Gardner are right. Man is both libidinous and social. At Color Research Institute we see no reason for discounting Freud's discoveries of subconscious or unconscious libidinous urges or for minimizing social identification with its status seeking. We operate on the assumption that man is both libidinous and social, that he has been conditioned by his parents and by his social group. The individual is motivated by pleasure drives and ego-involvement and is also motivated by social pressure and prestige identification.

In *The Lonely Crowd* by David Riesman, Nathan Glazer and Reuel Denney, it is stated that there can be no such thing as a society or a person wholly dependent on tradition-direction, inner-direction, or other-direction; each of these modes of conformity is universal.

It is being unrealistic to consider status symbols more important than sexual symbols or vice-versa. David Riesman's "other-directed" person may under some circumstances be "inner-directed" by some very deep-seated feeling or complex. However, many a habit established in early childhood is overwhelmed by social pressures and by the desire and drive for social status.

The "other-directed" person is constantly seeking something that is like that of his neighbors or that which has the highest social approval.

The "inner-directed" person wants French Provincial furniture not because it is traditional or has social status, but because in his childhood he and his parents were comfortable in a French Provincial environment.

Every realistic sociologist knows the reality of tradition-direction. New social concepts, new economic principles and new products are resisted by those who are "tradition-directed."

Without doubt, Riesman is right in his conclusion that people, particularly Americans, have become more status conscious, or as he puts it, more "other-directed" than people have been in other societies.

In dealing with people as consumers, we find that human beings in general are "tradition-directed," "inner-directed," and "other-directed."

In fact, we are not concerned either with the psychological or with the social problems of the respondents in our tests. We are interested only in their true attitudes and actual preferences. We seek to learn through the tests what motivates them to accept a product or brand or what causes them to reject it.

We classify consumers into social groups because we learned from sociology that there are differences in attitudes and preferences between different social groups. Our sociological considerations go no further.

As for Freudian contributions, we are indebted to psychoanalysis because it is this field of psychology that has made us aware of the unconscious mind and unconscious motivations and has taught us some of the ways of probing into the unconscious realm. We have no other interest in psychoanalysis. We are not in the sphere of measuring the emotional stability or the psychological character of an individual.

We are interested only in how a sample of consumers reacts to a specific stimulus (image, color, package, ad, name, etc.) Individuals are motivated by irrational elements but they try to give rational answers to questions about their attitudes and actions. Because individuals cannot or will not, tell us their real attitudes and actual preferences, we have to use means for getting their unconscious expressions or unguarded reactions. Our activities have no further relationship to psychoanalysis.

We use testing methods and techniques that originated in psychoanalysis, and employ controls that are necessary in all scientific investigations. We sample, or choose representative consumers of the product according to sociological standards.

Most of our tests are of the association-type and were first used in psychoanalysis. We use the semantic differential as a measuring instrument. It is in the realm of sociology and includes statistics. We choose our consumer samples according to social status, economic position, education, etc. These are in the sphere of sociology. We use controls in the design and the administration of the tests and use statistical structures.

We are not psychoanalysts, not mathematicians, not sociologists. We are market researchers who use modern testing methods and controlled techniques for learning how people react to a marketing tool or to a product.

gists. We are market researchers who use modern testing methods and controlled techniques for learning how people react to a marketing tool or to a product.

It should be obvious that individuals are motivated both socially and libidinously. Some persons are more libidinous than social; others are more social than libidinous. The same person is sometimes motivated socially and at other times libidinously. The following are examples of "libidinous" and "status" individuals.

About forty years ago, I knew a man who had a beautiful wife whom he literally kept under "lock and key." She was not permitted to go anywhere without him and they spent their vacations in places where he was sure he would not meet people who knew him. She wore the most unattractive dresses and tailored suits, but he bought her the most attractive, luxurious and costly underwear and night gowns. His wife was for him to enjoy, for no one else. I knew the secret of the beautiful intimate garments because I was privileged by the fact that I was only ten years old.

Another man I knew had a large and valuable collection of antique art. Every day he spent about two hours admiring and handling pieces of his collection. No one was ever invited to see the collection, not even members of his family were permitted into his private gallery.

Both of these are examples of individuals who were abnormally libidinous.

I knew a man who had no love for his wife, nor for his family. He enjoyed being away from his home and sought the company of other women indiscriminately, but he was very attentive to the "social needs of his family." His wife had a mink stole and a mink coat. She had her own luxury car, and the children were sent to private schools. "Social status" meant everything to this man. Almost everything he bought was for maintaining social status.

Another man I knew collected art. He bought old masters. He had Rembrandts and at least one Rubens. Several Venetian paintings were in his collection. Twice a year his gallery was open to the public and many came to see his art collection from all parts of the country and from foreign lands. He had no love for the paintings. Much to my surprise, I found out one day that he did not know one painting from another. The art collection had "social status" to him, but gave him no aesthetic pleasure whatever. The art collection merely served as a "symbol" that he was a financial success.

Most people do not behave in such extreme fashion. The majority of men and women have a little libido and some "status" craving. Normally a man or woman wants some pleasure, some sheer personal enjoyment and at other times some social approval and even applause.

Research objectivity is endangered when a researcher specializes in and concentrates on one of the behavioral sciences. The specialist often seeks only that which fits his specialty and therefore frequently fails to find the actual source of the trouble.

The research traditionalists use a mathematically precise statistical structure, beginning with random sampling and ending with statistics on areas sampled, social strata, economic status, education, etc. All this statistical structure, mathematically precise, is placed on a foundation consisting of consumers' verbalisms which are like shifting sands. Under these sand-like verbalisms are hidden all sorts of attitudes which do not reveal themselves in the verbalisms.

The motivation researchers, who rely on depth interviews and other unstructured testing techniques, have no research structure that can stand up and be measured. Yet they build their flimsy "idea tents" on the solid foundation of the unconscious mind, which is where the motivating force lies hidden.

However, marketing people need not depend either on a big solid looking statistical structure with a weak foundation or a strong foundation with a flimsy "idea tent." There is research that probes the unconscious motives with controlled, precise measuring instruments. There is research that makes use of a number of testing devices so that one can be used as a check on the other, just as in bookkeeping and accounting addition is used to check subtraction and subtraction is used to check addition.

Motivation research in which controlled testing techniques are used, is simple and basic. It is as simple and basic as addition and subtraction. There are ways of having representative consumers respond without their being on the defensive. There are methods for making respondents feel at ease. There are devices for giving the respondents a feeling of self-interest. There are procedures for getting the full and enthusiastic cooperation of representative individuals of potential consumers. There are means for motivating respondents.

Color Research Institute is one organization that tests marketing tools with controlled tests on an unconscious level. The following is a description of its services and procedures.

For determining "impact" of ads, an eye-movement test is used. This test is conducted with an instrument that produces a graph of the eye-flow of the respondents and shows the length of time the eyes rest on each focal point.

For determining the "impact" or display effectiveness of a package, three ocular measurements are made. An eye-movement test reveals the eye-flow and attention-holding power of the package. The two other ocular measurements are visibility of the package as a whole and readability of important copy on the package—brand name, product name, etc.

The ocular measurements show what consumers see on the package or perhaps, more precisely, what they look at, on the package. Seeing in this realm does not mean perception. It merely means sensation, attraction or attention-getting, with or without association. The package being seen merely means being noticed. It does not mean being understood, being liked or being accepted.

An eye-movement test by itself reveals much about the display value of the package. In conjunction with visibility and readability tests, we get still more information about the display effectiveness of the package. The ocular tests are conducted in a store set-up or marketing situation.

The visibility and readability are important because in the super market the package has to fight for attention. Whether the shopper sees the particular package on the shelf is involuntary on his or her part. Packages have varied degrees of attraction-getting and attention-holding power. Before the package can be liked or disliked it has to be seen and the brand name read.

The ocular measurements are vital because they show the involuntary reactions of consumers to the package. They reveal the display effectiveness of the package.

If the eye-movement test of the ad is favorable, if the ocular measurements of the package are favorable, then the marketing tool is put into field tests with several hundred consumers, to determine attitudes and preferences. For a national product, the sample is 800, 1,000 or 1,200 consumers in four, five or six parts of the country.

The basic field tests are controlled association tests. The subjects respond to the exhibit (ad, package, trademark, brand name or marketing theme) in terms of polar adjectives and with other specific associations provided in the test design. The tests reveal percentages of favorable attitudes, unfavorable attitudes and indifference. The measurement is in the semantic differential. Impact is shown in the total number of responses. (Subjects do not have to respond to all associations provided for them.)

The respondents do not know the objective of the test. The interviewer plays only a minor role in administering the test. The research is based on a system of testing, not on the skills of the interviewers.

Indirect preference tests and sensation transference tests are conducted in addition to association tests. The preference tests are indirect because they are designed and conducted so that the respondents are not aware that we are interested in their preferences. In the sensation-transference test, the subjects believe that the product is being tested. The well-known margarine and coffee tests, mentioned before and reported in detail in *How to Predict What People Will Buy*, are typical examples of sensation transference tests.

Ads as well as packages are tested by means of sensation transference tests. The product or package is tested without the ad and then it is tested in the presence of the ad. The test shows whether the ad upgrades or downgrades the brand, product or package. Some sensation-transference tests are visual, others involve the use of the product. In some cases, only the advertised brand is in the test. In others, a competitive product is included.

For testing cigarette ads, in some tests the subjects are asked to respond to the cigarette package and in other tests they are asked to smoke two cigarettes, one from the advertised package, another from a competitive package. Candy ad tests and some other food tests are also conducted either visually or by product taste or by product use.

Several controls are used in every field test. Each test is administered with an auxiliary test to which Color Research Institute has the answers. We know what the responses should be to this stimulus or exhibit, in the particular area, with the particular sample of consumers.

Usually the control test is on a color or design problem for the home. The control test serves three basic purposes. It is a subject designed to be of interest to the particular sample of consumers in order to get cooperative participation. It takes the commercial aspect away from the test so that the responses are natural, uninhibited, without defense mechanisms. We know what the answers to the control test should be from the particular sample of consumers. We thus use it as a control on sampling.

Another control is that a sample of 800 consumers involves eight field people. All the field people have to come up with the same scores, except for area deviation factors. An area deviation factor is the difference in attitude in an area to a given stimulus (color, image or design) from other areas. For example, we know that yellow has a 12% higher preference in Detroit than it does in New York. This also enables us to check on the sampling.

A third control is in that a minimum sample in each area is 200 consumers. Two field persons are always involved. Each handles 100 respondents. The results of the tests conducted by the two field people have to agree.

At the end of the association test comes the indirect preference test which is a fourth control. (The association test is always structured. In addition to polar terms, product-use and price associations are included. The association test discloses favorable and unfavorable attitudes or indifference.) The indirect preference test forces a decision or the making of a choice in which self-interest is involved.

A fifth control in keeping the test on an unconscious level is the fact that a color research institute, instead of a marketing research organization, is conducting the test.

The percentage of total favorable associations shows the degree of total favorable attitudes. An examination of the semantic differential in each pair of polar terms reveals percentages of specific favorable and unfavorable associations. For example, is the stimulus (package, ad, etc.) good only or is it also high quality, high price, pleasant and desirable?

Examination of the responses to the entire group of polar adjectives discloses the attitudes in depth. That is, do almost all the subjects respond to almost all the favorable terms, to almost all the unfavorable terms or is response light in both favorable and unfavorable associations, which means that many of the respondents are indifferent?

The indirect preference part of the test establishes the percentage of actual preference.

The eye-movement tests for measuring impact, eye-flow and attention-holding of ads, and the ocular measurements for determining impact, attention-getting, readability and display effectiveness of packages, take from a few days to one or two weeks to complete and are not costly because large samples of consumers are not involved.

Ocular measurements are of involuntary reactions which are generally the same with all individuals who have normal vision and are emotionally stable. Because the responses in these tests are instantaneous, associations are generally not involved. Therefore, ocular tests do not measure perception. They merely determine the kind and degree of attraction power.

Our field tests, that is, association-type and sensation-transference tests, with indirect preference tests, generally require from three to six weeks to complete and are relatively costly. However, they are not at all expensive when compared with depth interviews, and considering that for a national brand our samples range from 800 to 1200 consumers and for a regional brand 400 to 600 consumers.

There are two reasons why the controlled, structured association-type tests are actually not costly. The first is, they require only a few minutes to administer. The second is that controlled association tests based on the principle of the semantic differential produce clear-cut answers and there is no need for many highly trained, highly paid specialists to interpret the test results.

The results of such a test show clearly the percentage of total favorable and/or unfavorable attitudes, the kind and depth of favorable and/or unfavorable attitudes, the degree of interest or indifference and the percentage of preference with self-interest.

Color Research Institute offers still a third kind of service to its clients. It has extensive information on images and colors which is used as a basis for planning packages and for other design problems connected with marketing. This information on color and image preference (appeal), retention in the memory and on associations of specific images and colors, is based on tests that have been conducted with many thousands of individuals since 1935.

It would be neither practical nor ethical to conduct a field test to determine whether a specific red or a certain geometric image is a psychologically favorable element when we can go to our files and get information on the specific color (and often also on an image) based on tests conducted with from 50,000 to 150,000 individuals in over twenty years.

The file shows how the color or image rates in consumer acceptance, the specific associations that people have with it and how it rates in recall. It also reveals whether the consumer attitudes have been constant during the twenty years and whether the ratings are higher or lower now than they were twenty, ten or five years ago.

Taking advantage of this information saves much time which is always an important factor in marketing and the cost of this service is minimal.

I presume that there are other organizations who offer such services. Perhaps, there is no one other research organization offering all three services—ocular measurements, controlled field tests and image and color information based on accumulated data.

There must, however, be organizations who offer testing of marketing media with representative consumer samples, who measure actual motivations, not verbalisms, who use controls to assure that the responses are natural, real and indicative of consumer behavior in the shopping situation. If there are not a number of such organizations now, there soon will be.

Readership interviews and playbacks are not measurements of normal consumer behavior. At best, they provide flimsy and fragmentary information about marketing tools. Basically, they measure only the conscious aspects of printed ads and filmed commercials. But we know now that most of the effect of advertising is on an unconscious level. Most people are not aware that they have been motivated by a particular ad or commercial, that the desire to buy a certain product was prompted by a specific commercial or ad. Readership interviews and playbacks cannot possibly reveal the effect on the unconscious mind.

Individuals cannot tell about what they are not aware of having seen.

Motivation research that is based on depth interviews, on projective tests or on any unstructured, uncontrolled testing methods, is often very useful in pilot testing new ideas. Psychological probing by an expert can disclose much useful information. Obviously, both Ernest Dichter and Burleigh Gardner have made significant contributions to marketing by probing unconscious motivations and evaluating consumer behavior. The studies of motivations by specialists are a great improvement on head counting and statistics based on verbalisms. However, depth interviews and other unstructured, uncontrolled tests are not measurements.

Summing up package testing: before anything else, a package has to attract attention. The degree of attention-getting power is determined by means of a visibility measurement made with an optical instrument. This measurement reveals how or to what extent the package as a whole is seen from the shelf in comparison with competitive packages.

A second element that is vital is the readability of the brand name. Its readability is measured in the same way with the same type of instrument that is used to measure the package as a whole.

A third important factor is the "eye-flow," the way the eye travels across the surface of the package, where attention is held and where it is not held. This is determined by means of an eye-movement test with an eye-movement recording instrument.

The three tests measure the involuntary reactions to the package and reveal the display effectiveness of the package. After the display effectiveness has been found to be satisfactory, we proceed to get measurements of the psychological effect of components of the package and of the package as a whole.

Images, abstract or realistic, are psychological factors. The image that plays a role in identifying a package is a vital element on the package. We, therefore, establish the degree of appeal the image has, the associations it has and how it rates in retention in the memory.

The dominant color is also an important factor in the marketing effectiveness of the package. We, therefore, get preference (appeal), association, and retention in the memory ratings of the color or colors by which the package is identified.

Finally, the effect of the package as a whole is determined. This has to be established because the whole is different from, or more/or less than, the sum of its parts.

The psychological effect of an image, a color or the package as a whole is determined by means of controlled-association tests. These tests reveal the percentage of favorable response and degree of consumer interest. The tests disclose consumer attitudes toward the product in the package by means of specific favorable and/or unfavorable associations.

An indirect preference test is conducted in conjunction with the association test. It is indirect because the respondents are not aware that we are interested in their choices. The preference is expressed by the consumer on the basis of self-interest.

The indirect preference part of the test reveals the percentage of individuals in the consumer sample who actually want the product. The association part of the test discloses the specific reasons for their preference.

In testing the effectiveness of a package, the respondents are asked to respond to the product, that is, to the contents, not to the package. Consumers are not aware that they are influenced by a package and they do not consider the package important. Unconsciously they transfer the effect of the package to the product in it. Thus, an effective package communicates to the shopper that the product in the package is of high quality, whereas a "poor" package tells the shopper that the product it contains is of poor quality.

Summing up ad testing: first of all, the ad is put through an eye-movement test. If the eye-flow and attention-holding are favorable, the ad is tested in the field by means of an association test and/or a sensation-transference test.

We now have the means for predicting the behavior of consumers in relation to a specific product, package, marketing theme, printed ad or filmed commercial. We conduct controlled, structured tests that reveal true attitudes of consumers to a specific product or marketing tool and show actual consumer preference. These controlled tests are in statistical form. They are scientifically controlled measurements of consumer attitudes and behavior.

In dealing with the world of the atom, scientists cannot predict the behavior of a single electron. They must deal with many electrons in order to define their actions. The behavior of human beings is like that of electrons. Market researchers cannot predict the behavior of a single consumer, but by testing with a sample of several hundred consumers, they can predict the pattern of behavior of all potential consumers.

In business, statistical methods need no longer be limited to production, traffic control and insurance. Psychological testing techniques no longer are confined to psychotherapy. Scientific controls are now used in market testing as well as in the physics laboratory.

Fourteen years' experience of testing marketing media on an unconscious level under controlled conditions has demonstrated the validity of such tests. Many of the marketing successes that have been predicted by controlled tests conducted on an unconscious level are reported in *How to Predict What People Will Buy*.

Scientific marketing means marketing based on facts. It means that management makes decisions on the basis of objective information that can be acquired by scientifically controlled market testing.

Testing marketing media on an unconscious level by means of structured, controlled tests is scientific marketing research. It is scientific because it employs controls and reveals true consumer attitudes and actual consumer behavior in relation to the particular product or to the marketing tool that is being tested.

THE SEMANTIC DIFFERENTIAL AS A MEASURING INSTRUMENT

CLIENTS of Color Research Institute and others who have seen reports of their tests are familiar with controlled association tests that are based on the principle of the semantic differential.

In a controlled association test, polar terms or adjectives that represent attitudes are used. Examples of polar terms are good, bad; high quality, low quality; hot, cold; appealing, unappealing.

In association tests that are designed to measure judgment, a scale of several positions is used between each pair of terms for the respondent to indicate the intensity or depth of the judgment. The scale between bad and good, for example, may show whether in the individual's judgment the object is bad, a little bad, good, or almost good. This is a four-point scale. There can be a three-point scale, five-point scale, six, seven or still larger scale. When an individual judges an object or an idea against a series of scales, each judgment represents a selection from a set of alternatives. These judgments indicate intensity or degree of quality as well as direction.

An odd number of positions is generally used for measuring judgment. Three, five, seven, nine or eleven-point scales provide a middle position which is a neutral one. The semantic differential is in the scaling of the polar terms.

For example: *Detergent X*

	1	2	3	4	5	
high quality	X					low quality
for delicate garments		X				for work clothes
easy on hands				X		hard on hands

The above shows how the quality of each judgment is indicated by the position checked. Whether a three, five, seven, nine, eleven or still greater point scale is used depends on the problem and on the administrator of the test.

At Color Research Institute we measure attitudes, spontaneous, uninhibited reactions, not judgments which incorporate the wish to appear rational on the part of the respondent and in which various other conscious factors, unrelated to actual preference, play their parts.

Association tests are designed to reveal the unconscious reactions of the respondents. Such reactions can be obtained only if the respondents are asked to react quickly, not to judge. The tests have to be equal to actual marketing conditions or shopping situations, in which only acceptance or rejection is involved. They are therefore designed to disclose the percentage of favorable attitudes and percentage of unfavorable attitudes. A neutral position is indicated by no response.

In tests administered by Color Research Institute, the subjects do not have to respond to each pair of polar terms. Lack of response reveals indifference.

Charles E. Osgood, George J. Suci and Percy H, Tannenbaum of the Institute of Communications Research, University of Illinois, are the authors of *The Measurement of Meaning*, a book published by the University of Illinois Press in 1957. The book is a collaborative effort by the three authors and by thirty or more colleagues and graduate students of the University of Illinois.

The book is a progress report of the work on the measurement of meaning, the nature of meaning in word association research. It covers about fifty studies that were made during a period of about six years, beginning sometime in 1950.

The authors deal with the theoretical conception of the nature of meaning as well as with techniques of measurement. It is a complex, laboriously written and difficult to read volume. But it is of considerable significance to the marketing research field and particularly to those who are active in the fields of communication, public relations, advertising and marketing.

Following are some of the highlights from the book:

> Words represent things because they produce in human organisms some replica of the actual behavior toward these things, as a mediation process. This is the crucial identification, the mechanism that ties particular signs to particular significates rather than others. Stating the proposition formally: A pattern of stimulation which is not the significate is a sign of that significate if it evokes in the organism a mediating process, this process (a) being some fractional part of the total behavior elicited by the significate and (b) producing responses which would not occur without the previous contiguity of non-significate and significate patterns of stimulation. It will be noted that in this statement -we have chosen the term 'mediating process' rather than 'mediating reaction'; this is to leave explicitly open the question of the underlying nature of such representational mediators—they may well be purely neural events rather than actual muscular contractions or glandular secretions in the traditional sense of 'reaction.' In any case, in the formal statement of the theory they are presumed to have all the functional properties of stimulus-producing reactions.

The authors point out that words are signs and the most common verbal signs are highly similar. For example "sweet" is used and heard in the same way regardless of the cultural background of the individual. On the other hand, the meanings of many signs reflect the personal characteristics of the individual. For example, the meaning of "father," "mother," and "me" is not the same for persons who come from a normal versus an abnormal home environment.

The authors state that they wished to find a measurable activity or behavior of sign-using organisms which depends mostly on meaning and very little on other variables.

The search for such indices of meaning, while never very extensive and often inadvertent, has followed a number of different directions. These may be classified as physiological methods, learning methods, perceptual methods, association methods and scaling methods. They may be evaluated against the visual criteria for measuring instruments: (1) *Objectivity*. The method should yield verifiable, reproducible data which are independent of the idiosyncrasies of the investigator. (2) *Reliability*. It should yield the same values within acceptable margins of error when the same conditions are duplicated. (3) *Validity*. The data obtained should be demonstrably covariant with those obtained with some other, independent index of meaning. (4) *Sensitivity*. The method should yield differentiations commensurate with the natural units of the material being studied, i.e., should be able to reflect as fine distinctions in meaning as are typically made in communicating. (5) *Comparability*. The method should be applicable to a wide range of phenomena in the field, making possible comparisons among different individuals and groups, among different concepts and so on. (6) *Utility*. It should yield information relevant to contemporary theoretical and practical issues in an efficient manner, i.e., it should not be so cumbersome and laborious as to prohibit collection of data at a reasonable rate. This is not an exhaustive list of criteria of measurement, but it is sufficient for our purposes.

The authors say that this is not an exhaustive list of criteria. Although the rest of the book promises to be exhausting for the reader, this list of criteria should have great meaning to every serious, conscientious researcher.

The authors discuss in brief some of John B. Watson's Behaviorist theory, they sketch Galvanic Skin Response and Salivary Reaction and they conclude that these physiological methods are of dubious validity.

They discuss learning methods. "Semantic Generalization: Generalization is greater between semantically related words (e.g. style and fashion) than between phonetically related words (e.g. style and stile)."

Transfer and Interference Studies: "There is less interference among similar meaningful responses than among unrelated meaningful responses in the successive learning of lists of paired associates. There is a reciprocal inhibition operating between meaningfully opposed responses in such lists, the learning of one verbal response tending to block or decrease the speed of responding with the opposite verbal response to the same stimulus."

Perceptual Methods are discussed briefly and meaninglessly. However, it is pointed out that perceptual methods do not index the meaning.

Then Association-Testing Methods are covered. The authors point out that free association is actually not free because it is semantically determined. There are differences in specific meaning of the same word to different individuals. Associations to words describing objects are not the same as associations to the objects themselves. For example, words describing colors and colored objects do not always bring out the same associations. Associations to the word red may not be the same as associations to a red paper or a red box. Also, the "context" is important. The associations to a red paper, to a red box and to a red label on a can of vegetables may be totally different. The last example is mine.

The authors point out further that free association does not provide an index of the meaning because it lacks comparability. The responses of two individuals to the same stimulus, or of the same individual to two stimulus words, are unique, different.

Furthermore, free associations may be opposites. For example, white is frequently associated with black, bread is often associated with butter and man is normally associated with woman. These associations cannot be equated with meaning as can associations such as white with light and black with dark.

Now the authors enter the area of the Semantic Differential. After a brief discussion of Language as an Index of Meaning, the authors point out that unrestricted linguistic output has high presumptive validity, unless we question the honesty of the subject.

Up to this point, the authors quoted many important and unimportant studies. When they state that the honesty of the respondent is the only factor that diminishes the chances of validity, they reveal a lack of familiarity with the significant revelations in the literature of psychoanalysis.

Many psychological studies have demonstrated that defense mechanisms of respondents, "ego-involvement" factors and "prestige identification" elements, are more common than dishonesty. We have evidence that individuals are usually not aware that the answers they give are not indicative of how they will behave.

When an individual gives an answer consciously designed to put himself in a favorable light, he does not feel that he is being dishonest. Nor would the members of his social group consider him dishonest because he wants to make a favorable impression.

I question the validity of the studies covered in the book because of the failure to take into consideration the unconscious as well as conscious defense mechanisms of the respondents.

However, the authors demonstrate various phases of the measurement of meaning by the semantic differential.

They point out that a series of alternative verbal terms has to be devised. The respondents are not asked to give or emit associations. They are merely asked to select alternatives among successive pairs of verbal opposites. The selection isolates the meaning of the stimulus (object) or stimulus sign (word).

The authors also explain that in order to increase the sensitivity, they insert a scale between each pair of terms, so that the respondent can indicate both the direction and the intensity of each judgment.

Here again the authors reveal a lack of familiarity with psychoanalytical principles and lack of experience in the use of the semantic differential in solving practical marketing problems.

The semantic differential is based on a system of controlled association. The selection of polar terms is of vital importance. It has to be representative of all meanings. Synonyms are used in order to cover all possible interpretations.

Studies of the unconscious mind have shown that association tests, controlled or free, should be conducted so that responses are spontaneous, so that there is no time for defense mechanisms to get into the test situation.

The studies have shown that controlled association tests are remarkably effective tools for measuring attitudes, unconscious reactions, not for eliciting judgments or for measuring intensity of each judgment.

The moment an individual is asked to judge and to reveal his judgment, his defense mechanisms are immediately called into action. Ego-involvement and prestige identification immediately enter the test situation. Guards that operate both on a conscious and on an unconscious level take over the duties of protecting the ego and of maintaining its privacy.

Furthermore, in solving practical marketing problems we are not concerned with the intensity of judgment of an individual. For example, in the super market the problem is not whether the shopper likes a package or brand very much, much, a little or very little. The question is whether she likes it or does not like it; whether she will take it home or will not take it home.

In solving practical problems we are, therefore, interested in black or white answers. The controlled association test is by its basic nature a black or white test. The bipolar adjectives are positive or negative. The tests can be conducted, and they have been for more than a dozen years at Color Research Institute, so that the responses are spontaneous and natural, revealing deep-seated attitudes, true feelings, not judgments.

However, the controlled association tests do reveal depth and intensity in the number of responses. In these tests, respondents do not have to react in every way indicated by the selected polar adjectives or other terms. The test reveals percentage of favorable responses, unfavorable responses and indifference.

Any stimulus (package, ad, image or color) may evoke mostly favorable responses, mostly unfavorable reactions or neither favorable nor unfavorable attitudes. A stimulus that evokes neither favorable nor unfavorable responses from a large number of persons is a weak stimulus. It is assumed to lack impact and therefore is a weak medium of communication.

The total number of responses in a controlled association test of a marketing tool reveals the effectiveness of the marketing tool in depth. In other words, the degree of impact the package (ad or other marketing tool being tested) has is revealed in the total number of responses.

The qualitative effect of the stimulus (package or other marketing tool) is disclosed in the semantic differential, in the number of favorable and number of unfavorable associations.

The semantic differential in controlled association tests has been used by us for over twelve years as a means of measuring the marketing effectiveness of various types of marketing tools—advertising themes, brand images, brand names, packages, ads, etc.

The authors of *The Measurement of Meaning* report the use of a seven-step scale for the respondent to indicate the intensity of his judgment. Various scales have been used for measuring intensity of individual response in experimental studies that were conducted under my direction during the period of 1935–1940, under the auspices of the Adult Education Program of the Chicago Board of Education.

We found very soon, after having had only a few experiences in trying to solve practical marketing problems, that the depth of judgment of the individual is of no practical value and that allowing time for judgment meant allowing time to call forth defense mechanisms. Thus natural feelings and true attitudes did not reveal themselves in the tests.

The semantic differential of a controlled association test that is designed and conducted to evoke spontaneous responses is an objective measurement. The objectivity is maintained in the analysis of the test results. Subjectivity of an individual who interprets the results plays a very small role because the results are explicit.

The reliability of this system of testing attitudes is demonstrated by the fact that the same scores can be reproduced when the same objects are measured with several matched samples of respondents. For example, if a package has 75% total favorable associations with a sampling of 600 respondents of a lower middle socioeconomic classification, the package will have about 75% favorable associations if it is tested with an additional sampling of 600 respondents of the same lower middle socio-economic classification.

The validity of the semantic differential system of measurement in controlled association tests is now evident. The criteria are in the sales results. For nearly fifteen years, controlled association tests have been used as a basis for executive judgment in making marketing decisions on many well-known brands. The marketing successes have been reported in a number of articles and in my book, *How to Predict What People Will Buy*.

After covering many pages discussing scales, graphs, scores and factor analysis, the authors of *The Measurement of Meaning* discuss meaning versus attitude in the prediction of behavior. They point out that attitude scales or measurements alone do not provide a basis for predicting behavior in actual situations. Specific attitudes indicate specific behavior under the same conditions. Favorable attitudes toward an object under one condition are not necessarily the same under different conditions. Studies conducted by Color Research Institute have demonstrated this to be true.

First example: An association test report (consisting of a series of polar adjectives) showed that a certain packaged food product rated 80% in favorable associations. The indirect preference test that followed, with the same sample of consumers, showed that the preference rating was only 74%. In other words, 6% of the respondents did not want the product for one reason or another, although they had favorable attitudes toward it. Some may have had the product. Others may have had a similar product toward which their attitudes were equally favorable.

Second example: a well-known product in a new package received 84% favorable associations when tested by itself. When it was tested against the old package, it received 64% favorable associations and the old package had 36%. When the new package was tested by itself, it was consciously or unconsciously compared with other brands. In the direct-comparison test, the brand was not a factor. The packages differed only in design.

The chapter in *The Measurement of Meaning* on Studies in Color Meanings was of great interest to me because of the similarity of the testing situation and the findings to the studies I conducted with color in 1935–1940.

In the description of the color tests the authors reveal an awareness of the importance that the element being tested should not be revealed to the respondents. Finding this was a pleasant surprise, because in the discussion of theory and testing principles the authors do not cover behavior on an unconscious level and the

LOUIS CHESKIN

necessity of testing on an unconscious level.

The authors report that an ad of a known brand was produced in several color combinations. The color of the product shown on the ad and the background of the ad were different in each. Six groups of 20 individuals each were used in the test. Each group was exposed once to each of the color combinations of the ad. The individuals were asked to judge the product itself against a set of 20 semantic seven-point differential scales. No reference to the color was made.

There is no value in quoting the results of this experiment. Six samples of 20 are not large enough, even when students are used as subjects. A group of 20 may consist of men and/or women. They may be first, second, third and fourth year students, or a few or all may be graduate students. Sampling is very important where color meanings are concerned.

Still more important, a seven evaluative scale of judgment of colors has little to do with actual attitudes toward colors. A number of studies I conducted in 1935–1940 and in 1945–1947 show that most normal individuals react to primary and secondary hues positively or negatively, favorably or unfavorably, not in depth. An individual either likes blue or he does not like it. He likes red or he doesn't. However, to tints, shades and tones, individuals react in depth, that is, a person will like a light blue a little more or a little less than a darker blue or a still lighter blue. These studies are reported in "Indirect Approach to Market Reactions," *Harvard Business Review*, September, 1948, and in *How to Predict What People Will Buy*.

However, the studies in color meanings reported in *The Measurement of Meaning* are significant because they show an awareness of the "unconscious level" factor, in the fact that the respondents were asked to judge the product, as such, without reference to the color.

Studies of this type are called "sensation transference" tests at Color Research Institute.

Example: The problem is to determine which of two package designs is the more effective marketing tool. When the association test, mainly consisting of polar adjectives, is being conducted, it is implied that the products in the two packages are different. Actually they are identical. Generally, most respondents believe the two products to be different because they transfer the sensation from the package to the product. This transference is unconscious. In some tests the individuals are asked to use the product or to taste it. Other tests are visual.

Some of the findings of the three authors about the effects of colors upon the "evaluation" of objects with which they are associated are valid. The studies showed that regardless of the object with which the colors were associated, reds were associated with "activity" and blues with "passivity." In general, the authors report that they found the objects with highly saturated (intense) colors were judged to be more potent than the same objects with colors of low saturation. The authors declare: "Parallelisms between meaningful connotations and the hue and saturation of colors may well be general cross-culturally. Research is now under way to check this possibility."

While this experimental research is under way, there are in the files of Color Research Institute many more than a hundred studies showing conclusively that hue and degrees of saturation have the same connotations of degree of activity or potency to all cultural levels and across all socio-economic strata. However, attitudes toward all colors, saturated and unsaturated, and color preferences are totally different in different cultural levels or social groups. I have reported the results of many of these studies. (*Colors: What They Can Do for You*, 1947–8; *Color for Profit*, 1951; *Color Guide for Marketing Media*, 1954; *How to Color-Tune Your Home*, 1954.)

The chapter dealing with studies on advertising is directly related to much of the work at Color Research Institute. It is therefore appropriate for me to review this chapter here. One study reported was conducted by Mindak in 1955. The purpose of the study was to measure the effectiveness of five different types of radio appeals dealing with a new hand lotion. There were five one-minute radio commercials with the following appeals: 1) negative appeal (emphasis on symptoms of cracked skin, calloused hands, etc.); 2) testimonial appeal (Marilyn Monroe suggests use of the product because of her own personal success with it); 3) scientific appeal (emphasis on the scientific newness of the product, using several pseudo-scientific terms); 4) "romance despite work" appeal (emphasis on maintaining lovely hands despite their use in household tasks); and 5) the "zany" appeal (whimsical appeal with considerable use of puns). Each of these five versions was used at the opening and closing of a fifteen minute musical comedy. An eight-scale differential was used.

The results showed that each of the five appeals produced significant change in attitudes toward the product. The scientific appeal was the only one that changed the attitudes in a favorable direction. All the other four appeals produced unfavorable changes. The testimonial appeal produced the biggest negative change.

The sample of respondents cannot be considered a normal one. The subjects were female undergraduates who should not be expected to be impressed by Marilyn Monroe.

Because of the use of an eight-scale differential, the respondents acted as judges or critics not as consumers normally act. Under natural conditions in daily life, the individuals would react either favorably or unfavorably or they would be indifferent to the commercial.

The results from an eight-scale differential cannot be used to predict behavior in a real marketing situation because eight-scale judgments are almost non-existent in actual daily life.

The Measurement of Meaning is not a book containing anything that is new in research. It deals with cases that are almost entirely experimental. The authors neglected the wealth of information they could have obtained from the literature in the field of psychoanalysis. The unconscious mind is given little consideration.

The authors dwell mostly on the structure of semantic differential measurement. "Ego-involvement," "prestige identification" factors and other defense mechanisms which enter every testing situation, unless controls are used, are given no attention. The emphasis is on judgments in which defense mechanisms are involved, not on unconscious reactions of the subjects. The experiments that are reported do not have standards that can be used in solving actual marketing problems.

In spite of these limitations and the laboriously written, academic, dry and difficult to read style, *The Measurement of Meaning* is an important book because it sets forth many of the advantages of the Semantic Differential as a measuring instrument. It contains excellent discussions on the use of polar terms. It presents considerable information on many studies in the field of controlled association testing.

CHAPTER 9

HOW SCIENTIFIC CAN MARKETING RESEARCH BE?

MANY company managers and advertising executives have little or no confidence at all in marketing research. Some agree to conducting research on a specific problem of marketing or advertising. If the results confirm their personal beliefs, the research is accepted. If the results contradict the personal opinion of the president, brand manager or advertising executive, whoever is in the position to make the decision, the research is disregarded.

Marketing managers and advertising executives have no confidence in research because they have seen marketing programs, advertising campaigns and individual ads that came out with high scores in the tests fail in the market.

The reason that research did not predict consumer behavior is not the failure of research, but the failure of the particular kind of research, the wrong kind, for solving the particular problem.

Marketing managers and advertising executives who are aware of the following will not have the occasions to blame research for failure. Research that measures ads on the basis of conscious recall of potential consumers does not reveal the effectiveness of the ads. Research that records what people say is not the same as recording how people feel. Research that is conducted without controls is not reliable research.

Furthermore, no matter what you have to sell, you can't sell to everyone. You may be able to get 5% of the market or 50%, but you will never get 100% or anywhere near it. If you have research conducted with consumers in a high income, high education level, and your market is in the low income, little education strata, the research is worthless no matter how well the tests were controlled and how much the responses represent actual attitudes. A test will not reveal attitudes of potential consumers if cake mixes are tested with samplings of college students.

The kind of marketing tests that are reliable, dependable guides to marketing success have already been discussed. Store audits, such as are conducted by A. C. Nielsen, are as reliable as the organization with its facilities and controls makes them. Nielsen services have proved their value.

In the area of predicting consumer behavior, the research has to measure attitudes, true attitudes, not verbalisms, and actual preference in which self-interest is involved. Marketing research, like all research, incorporates principles, systems, controls and objectives. The measuring instrument is a factor in the research results, of any kind of research, in every field, whether it is in marketing or in physics.

There are still many in the marketing and advertising fields who do not realize that marketing research can be "scientific" and that marketing as a whole should be "scientific."

Prejudice against "scientific" marketing is demonstrated by the following statement which appeared in the November 3, 1958, issue of *Advertising Age.* "I don't think marketing research is worth a damn—and furthermore, I don't think there is such a thing as merchandising," said Benedict Gimbel Jr., President and General Manager of WIP (Radio) in Philadelphia.

He went on to say that economic factors are the "direct result of individual human behavior and are not in any way predictable."

Mr. Gimbel cited the Hula Hoop craze as not being predictable and the "chrome" on cars that people did not want but surveys showed they wanted. He also ridiculed the research of a very successful brand of cigarettes.

"Play your hunches, trust your instincts," Mr. Gimbel said.

Mr. Gimbel's statements don't even fit the age of pre-atomic, classical, Newtonian science. They are more in the realm of the Stone Age. The examples he gives do not prove his statements at all.

There was no capital investment made on manufacturing the material for Hula Hoops. The material used was originally made for other purposes. The Hula Hoops were tested in a small community before quantity manufacturing facilities were set up.

I have already discussed fully the marketing factors in Detroit. The auto makers are the best example of the wrong use of research. Car design preference cannot be determined by surveys.

The Marlboro ads were tested and the Marlboro package was developed on the basis of controlled tests. The final package was approved by management after extensive and thorough research, conducted on an unconscious level, showed that the package symbolized a masculine brand and had the connotations of a quality product. Almost a hundred package designs were tested before the final one was evolved.

I know this because I supervised the package tests and the ad tests that were conducted for the Philip Morris Company. I know also that the product itself was carefully tested by another research organization before management approved the blend of tobacco.

When I was a boy, I knew a man who said, whenever he had the opportunity, that there were only two ways of getting rich; one way is to have oil found on your land; the other way is to marry a girl on whose father's land oil was found. He was a sweet old man, but he did not contribute to my education. Mr. Gimbel reminds me of this man.

Scientific marketing has made great progress, in spite of the survival of Stone Age marketing notions. Among the leaders in scientific marketing is George Weissman. The following was reported in the same issue with Mr. Gimbel's "primitive" statement: "George Weissman, Vice President and Director of Marketing of Philip Morris Inc., told the meeting that a company such as Philip Morris, which has an integrated marketing structure, looks to an agency primarily for 'the finest creative efforts.'"

He explained, "that since his company is organized to handle marketing problems 'in depth,' it considers the marketing services of an agency 'supplementary.'"

"We desire a good creative agency and welcome the supplementary marketing services. We would not be interested in a good marketing agency with supplementary creative services," he said.

"Market planning and marketing research cannot be really 'scientific' like physics," a corporation president said to me recently, when I told him that there are tests for measuring consumer behavior which are just as scientific as tests in physics. "In physics, the scientists deal with absolute, natural laws, not with unpredictable human beings," he added. This attitude toward marketing research and this concept of physics or what has traditionally been considered science, is prevalent in marketing and advertising circles.

Many men in top management positions, a great number of department managers and most advertising executives, believe that there are "absolutes in science" but that they have to deal with "unpredictable human beings" in marketing and in marketing research. Therefore, they act on the assumption that the attitudes of potential customers are not measurable and markets are not predictable.

I present what a world famous physicist, winner of the Nobel Prize, has to say about physics, experiments in physics, theories and philosophies. I quote from the book, *Physics and Philosophy, The Revolution in Modern Science*, by Werner Heisenberg (Harper & Brothers, 1958).

Werner Heisenberg is director of the Max Planck Institute for Atomic Physics at Munich, Germany, and he is a scientific consultant to the West German Government. He has lectured in the United States. He worked with Niels Bohr in developing new principles in the quantum theory. He is recognized as one of the world's greatest atomic scientists.

"Everyone should understand the philosophy of the new physics" says F. S. C. Northrop, Professor of Philosophy and Law, Yale University, in his introduction in the book by Werner Heisenberg.

"The assumptions, or assumed theories, are philosophical in character," says Northrop.

Heisenberg points out that an attempt by Planck to reconcile his new hypothesis, that energy is emitted or absorbed in discrete energy quanta, with the older laws of radiation failed in the essential points.

Einstein made use of the new idea of energy in the well-known "photoelectric effect," the emission of electrons from metals under the influence of light. Experiments had shown that energy of the emitted electrons depended on the color or frequency, not on the intensity of the light. This could not be understood on the basis of the traditional theory of radiation. Einstein explained the observations by interpreting Planck's hypothesis to mean that light consists of quanta of energy traveling through space.

The traditional theory of the specific heat of solid bodies was also modified by Einstein who explained the behavior by applying the quantum hypothesis to the elastic vibrations of the atoms in the solid body.

Einstein showed that light could be interpreted as consisting of electromagnetic waves, according to the Maxwell theory, or as consisting of light quanta, energy packets traveling through space with high velocity.

Heisenberg says that Niels Bohr was aware that the quantum conditions are not consistent with Newtonian mechanics. In the case of the hydrogen atom, on the basis of Bohr's theory, the frequencies of the light emitted by the atom could be calculated to agree with observations. But the frequencies were different from the orbital frequencies of the electrons circling the nucleus. Bohr's theory was a combination of classical mechanics for the motion of the electrons with quantum conditions.

There were apparent contradictions between the results of different experiments. How does the same radiation that produces interference patterns, and therefore must consist of waves, also produce the photoelectric effect, and therefore must consist of moving particles?

Attempts to describe atomic events in the traditional terms of physics led to contradictions.

Bohr's theory, known as the Copenhagen interpretation of quantum theory, starts from a paradox.

Because a specific thing cannot be a particle (a substance confined to an extremely small volume) and a wave (a field spread out over a large space), the two are mutually exclusive but they complement each other. Bohr uses the concept of "complementarity" in the interpretation of quantum theory. "The knowledge of the position of a particle is complementary to the knowledge of its velocity or momentum. If we know the one with high accuracy we cannot know the other with high accuracy; still we must know both for determining the behavior of the system."

The theoretical interpretation of an experiment starts with two steps. In the first step we have to describe the arrangement of the experiment eventually combined with a first observation, in terms of classical physics. Then translate this description into a probability function that follows the laws of quantum theory. Then its change in the course of time, which is continuous, can be calculated from the first conditions.

Heisenberg points out that the probability function combines both objective and subjective elements. It contains statements about possibilities or tendencies, which are completely objective. They do not depend on any observer. It contains statements about our knowledge of the system, which are subjective because they may not be the same for different observers.

When we come to the second observation, the result of which should be predicted from the theory, it is vital to be aware that the object has to be in contact with the other part, which is the experimental arrangement, the measuring device or instrument, before or at the time of observation.

The probability function contains the objective element of tendency and the subjective element of incomplete knowledge. The observation itself changes the probability function discontinuously. In other words, the observation plays a decisive role in the event. The reality depends considerably on whether we observe it or not and on who the observer is.

Heisenberg says that we cannot know beforehand which limitations will be put on the applicability of certain concepts by the extension of our knowledge. Within the mathematical framework of Newtonian mechanics there were defined concepts and meanings. But in relation to nature, there are no well defined concepts.

Einstein's theory of special relativity led to the discovery of new properties of space and time, specifically of a relation between space and time that had not been known before and did not exist in Newtonian mechanics. The equivalence of mass and energy is the most important consequence of the principle of relativity. An atomic explosion demonstrates the correctness of Einstein's equation.

However, this discovery did not disprove Newtonian mechanics as some physicists first believed. It merely meant that wherever the concepts of Newtonian mechanics can be used to describe events in nature, the laws formulated by Newton are correct and cannot be improved. But the electromagnetic phenomena cannot adequately be described by the concepts of Newtonian mechanics. A system essentially different from it has to be used.

The theory of relativity is connected with a universal constant in nature, the velocity of light. This constant determines the relation between space and time. Planck's universal constant is the quantum of action.

Heisenberg points out that "science and art are not very different" and he discusses fully the philosophic aspects of science and the political aspects in the present social scene. He also traces the historical growth, the interdependence and interaction of science and philosophy.

The physicist uses a mathematical scheme for the interpretation of experiments. But he has to speak to nonphysicists in plain language, understandable to anybody. "Even to the physicist, the description in plain language will be a criterion of the degree of understanding that has been reached. Communication is a problem as much as physics" says Heisenberg.

In the last two chapters of the book, Heisenberg discusses the sociological aspects of physics and shows that the problems in physics are about the same as the problems in society.

"Objectivity," "subjectivity," "communication," "understanding," "open-mindedness," "philosophy," "principles," "systems," "known factors," "probabilities," "uncertainty," "measuring instruments," appear often in Werner Heisenberg's book, *Physics and Philosophy*.

Why do I devote so much space to physics in a book for businessmen and advertising people? One reason is that every intelligent person should know about this book, and I assume that anyone who reads *Why People Buy* is an intelligent individual. But primarily, my aim is to demonstrate that the problems of the marketing research field are no different from those in the field of physics. In marketing research, as in physics, we have problems of controls and communication and we deal with concepts, with known and unknown factors and with measuring instruments.

I considered this chapter finished at this point until I heard the following from a friend of mine who is an important executive and is classed as an intelligent man by me and by others. He said, "Heisenberg must be an eccentric among scientists," after hearing what I said about the new book, *Physics and Philosophy*.

Therefore, intelligent reader, I will quote from an article that appeared in the June, 1957, issue of the *Bulletin of the Atomic Scientists*. The article was written by Max Born, one of the founders of modern physics.

Says Born: "True science is philosophical; physics in particular, is not only a first step toward technology, but a way to the deepest layers of human thought. Just as three hundred years ago physical and astronomical discoveries dethroned medieval scholasticism and opened the way to a new philosophy, today we are witnessing a movement which, starting from apparently insignificant physical phenomena, leads to a new turn in philosophy."

He discusses further "calculus of probability" which is used in insurance, industrial production, regulation of traffic, as well as in astronomy, genetics and physics. He points out that statistical methods are used "to explain relationships between observable quantities, like density, pressure, temperature, which are averages; therefore, the Kinetic theory of gases was developed with the help of statistical methods, and out of this development grew the more general theory of statistical mechanics."

The laws of mechanics as founded by Galileo and Newton are strictly causal and deterministic. The movement of atoms in a gas is a process which combines regularity with randomness.

Max Born compares the movement of the atoms with a man in a community or state who follows the impulses of his will and is simultaneously subjected to the influences of his surroundings and of his neighbors.

"When we consider the behavior of a large number of men in a community, we will observe a mixture of psychological and statistical regularities which are analogous to those of statistical thermodynamics."

Max Born compares the development of science with the development of civilization and points out the statistical similarities between atoms and nations. Atomic physics has taught us not only things about the material world, but also a new way of thinking. It has given us a philosophy, a doctrine of living.

The original rigid causal laws of Newtonian mechanics had to be supplemented by probability considerations to permit the proper treatment of gases and other systems composed of many atoms.

Max Born says in this enlightening article that many scientists still thought that the particles, if only their movement could be observed in detail, would obey the same mechanical laws as do the planets, the positions of which can be predicted thousands of years ahead.

But as the investigation of the structure of the single atom progressed, it became clear that the electrons in the clouds surrounding the nucleus did not obey the classical laws of mechanics.

Planck's quantum theory, which was announced in 1900, was the basis for modern quantum mechanics which brought order and meaning into the chaos of atomic phenomena. "The new mechanics makes, in principle, only statements of probability. It does not answer the question, where a particle is at a given instant, but only the question, what the probability is for a particle being at a given time at a certain place."

This theory is based on the recognition that every observation implies an interference with, and a perturbation of, the thing that is observed.

The laws of nature prohibit absolute data to be used, as in classical mechanics, to predict the course of a movement of a particle.

The restriction of measurability is the essence of Heisenberg's "uncertainty principle."

Max Bom also discusses the "complementarity principle" of Niels Bohr which applies to two different aspects of the same physical situation, resulting from two different methods of observation.

Max Born points out that Bohr's "complementarity principle" applies to everyday life as well as to physics. He quotes Niels Bohr as saying: "It is the very difficulty of appreciating the traditions of other nations on the basis of one's own national tradition that requires that the relationship between cultures may rather be regarded as complementary." Niels Bohr, the great scientist and abstract thinker, urges free acknowledgment of being different and replacement of enmity between peoples by the sense of their complementarity.

Max Born says still more about the similarity between social problems and scientific problems. Clearly, he speaks the same language of science and society as Werner Heisenberg.

Because this book is a definitive one, I believe that marketing research should be shown against the background of social values. Marketing does not deal merely with the profit motive. Marketing has to do with the distribution and consumption of goods. It, therefore, is basically related to the social structure as a whole. Marketing research and research in the field of physics thus are related to life as a whole. For this reason, I will say a little more about the recent revolutionary changes in the basic concepts of the physical and social world.

We were taught at school that science concerns itself with the properties of inanimate matter and the laws which apply to it. Physics dealt with all the "real" things around us, except living organisms.

People are more aware of physics now than they were fifty years ago or even twenty years ago. They know that physics produces technical miracles, such as television, atom bombs, manmade satellites, cosmic rockets, and at the same time it deals with invisible entities and incredible properties.

Max Born says in another comprehensive article in the October, 1958, issue of the *Bulletin of the Atomic Scientists* that, in dealing with atomic systems, it is no longer possible to make statements of this kind: Under such and such conditions, this and this *will happen*. It is only possible to say: Under definite conditions there will be a definite *probability* that this and this will happen, another *probability* that that and that will happen, and so on. The predictions of the theory are not deterministic, but statistical, and they apply not to a supposedly objectively occurring process as such, but only to situations produced by conscious experimentation.

However, despite this entry of a subjective element into the study, each experiment provides a contribution to objective statements. It can be said—and it corresponds exactly to the mathematical structure of the theory—that every single experiment is a projection of reality.

Think, for example, of the elliptic shadow which a circular object such as a dinner plate throws on the wall. By observing this shadow, one obtains no convincing proof of the circular shape of the original object, or of its dimensions; this conclusion can be derived from observation of several such shadows on different walls. Each single shadow thus contains a contribution to the knowledge of reality, and a sufficiently large number of shadow-casting experiments conveys the complete reality. The latter is something invariant, independent of the projections.

Exactly the same thing is valid for atomic experiments and their quantum-mechanical interpretation. A single experiment provides, in general, no conclusive knowledge of reality. From a well-organized series of experiments, one can derive invariants, attributable to real things, exactly as the brain derives them, unconsciously, from nerve signals.

In pre-quantum days it could be imagined that one could try to improve (and actually improve) a single experiment so as to make it reveal the complete reality. One could, for example, throw simultaneously several shadows of the same plate on different walls and derive from this single experiment the shape and diameter of the plate.

Quantum mechanics says that the location and the velocity of an electron cannot be determined simultaneously and exactly. The more precisely one seeks to measure one of these magnitudes, the more uncertain the other becomes. This is Heisenberg's famous "uncertainty principle." The different situations created by experimentation are, as Niels Bohr says, "complementary."

Through systematic creation of conditions for the performance of different experiments, one can, however, again arrive at invariants, at common qualities and quantities.

The quantum theory provides us, by the intermediary of its invariants a picture of reality satisfying all reasonable needs.

Max Born points out further: "Chemistry believed in the permanence of elements, in their incapacity to change. Hydrogen and oxygen thus did have specific properties. Today this is an obsolete idea. All elements consist of the same ultimate components, nucleons and electrons, and can be converted into each other. There are no specific laws valid for a single atom any more; atoms of every kind are, in principle, describable through a solution of the general quantum-mechanical man-body problem.

"One could object that the elementary particles themselves, the nucleons and electrons, as well as photons, neutrons, mesons and hyperons, are now being characterized by specific relationships. This is obviously only a temporary state of science. Einstein, Eddington, and others attempted to develop a unified, all-inclusive theory. They failed, because they did not possess all the necessary empirical foundation for their theory. Today it is different.

"We now have a good general knowledge of elementary particles, of their properties and transformations; and the all-inclusive theory also may be already there: I mean the spin theory of elementary particles, recently announced by Heisenberg and Pauli. This theory has raised as much excitement among physicists in the Soviet Union as it did in the West. Physicists of the whole world understand each other well, despite differences of official ideologies.

"Distinctions based on the scheme 'materialism vs. idealism' do not correspond with the facts of our time."

Soviet scientists still claim that objective laws exist in society which are specific for a given society and independent of human conscience.

Says Max Born: "The principle of 'historical materialism" is the real root of the conflict between East and West, because it is the basis of the fanatic belief of Marxists that the world is bound to fall to them spontaneously and inevitably.

"This belief is a descendant of the physical determinism derived from Newtonian mechanics. There it looks as if the laws of nature should permit us to predict, with absolute certainty, all that is going to happen in the future, if only the initial state is fully known. In recent years I have made some effort to demonstrate the fallacy of this deterministic interpretation of classical mechanics and of the whole physics derived from it.

"The claim of Marxism to be a scientific interpretation of the world (in fact, the only valid scientific interpretation) represents a danger to mankind. A similar danger is the arrogance of the liberal capitalistic West, which calls itself Christian, but in its policies pays no attention to Christ's teachings. I do not believe that Jesus would have approved of defending Christianity with atom bombs."

Max Born hopes that physicists can make a contribution toward international understanding by renouncing the extreme idea of positivism (philosophical subjectivism or idealism) that dominates the Western countries, as well as of materialism that now dominates the Soviet Union and China. Above all, we must do away with the fairy tale of physical determinism and thus also with the specter of historical inevitability.

What does all this specifically have to do with marketing research? What Max Born says applies to marketing research.

As Werner Heisenberg and Max Bom point out, there is an element of indeterminacy in the universe of an atom which cannot be measured. Some elements act according to known physical laws. The movements of other elements are unpredictable.

A physicist cannot predict the behavior of a single electron because the means he uses for observing or measuring its behavior changes its course. Therefore, a physicist has to deal with great numbers of electrons in order to define their behavior.

Human beings behave like electrons. In some ways, the behavior of an individual is predictable. In some areas reactions of consumers follow known patterns of behavior. In other areas, particularly where the unconscious mind is involved, actions of individuals do not follow known behavior patterns. A market researcher cannot predict the behavior of a single consumer because the means the researcher uses for observing or measuring the behavior often changes the behavior. Therefore, a market researcher has to deal with a great number of potential consumers in order to predict their pattern of behavior.

In testing consumer attitudes, we have the problem of the interviewer (observer) who in some degree, very little or very much, affects the test. The bias of the one who executes the test may be insignificant or very significant, depending on the ways in which controls are used, in the test design and in its administration.

In depth interviewing, the bias of the interviewer or "observer," the subjective factor, may be very great because the interview is largely manipulated by the interviewer.

In controlled-association tests, the interviewer (observer) bias is minimized but never completely eliminated.

In sampling consumers we are dealing with "probability" and "uncertainty" (as in quantum physics).

The principle of "complementarity" shows up when we conduct two kinds of marketing tests with the same problem.

We often find contradictions in marketing research, as in physics, because two tests intended to measure the same thing actually measure two different things or two sides of the same thing.

In planning a marketing test we must give consideration to the "uncertainty" aspect. Where great numbers are involved the "probability" factor is for practical purposes insignificant.

What percentage is significant in marketing research? Is 5% a meaningful advantage? In a marketing test, does the advantage over a competitive product, package, ad, etc., have to be 10%, 25%, or more?

Assuming the test is controlled, that obvious bias has been eliminated, that the sample is representative of the potential consumers of the product, that the testing technique and procedure are valid and the persons conducting the tests are reliable, the size of the sample is a determinant of the per cent that should be considered significant.

If a 10% advantage represents 100 respondents or more, it is significant; if it represents 5 respondents, it has no significance. In other words, if with a sample of 1,000 consumers, one exhibit has 55% favorable associations and the other 45%, the 10% superiority is meaningful and indicative of consumer behavior. It indicates a definite probability that the product having 10% advantage in the test will have a similar advantage in the market, provided that other marketing factors remain approximately the same.

If the sample is only 100, a 10% advantage is not meaningful and with a sample of 50 respondents, a 10% advantage has even less meaning because the elements of "uncertainty" are too great about the behavior of a few individuals being indicative of general consumer behavior. On the basis of the results from a small sample or insufficient testing, it cannot be said that there is a definite "probability" that such and such will happen in the market.

The absolutes of "cause and effect" or of "determinism" are no longer here. We know now that events in nature are indeterminate and that the exact future is unpredictable. Physical science is not as precise as we thought it was.

While physical science has become "less precise" because of our increased knowledge, marketing and marketing research have become more precise because of the new knowledge. Max Born points out that statistical methods are used in all fields in which large numbers of units are involved—industrial production, traffic control and insurance, as well as in astronomy, genetics and physics.

The individual who believes that marketing is a hunch business or a guessing game and that physical science is absolute and precise should become interested in "Adult Education." The present-day business executive who does not know that marketing and marketing research can be "scientific" is losing money for his company and/or himself.

"Scientific" means measured with reliable instruments under controlled conditions. The attitudes of people toward anything— product, package, brand name, brand image, advertising theme, individual ad or filmed commercial—can be determined by employing controlled testing techniques.

For one who has been trained and conditioned to believe certain ideas or concepts to be true, it is difficult to accept the revelation that they have been proved false. Many physicists could not accept, and some still cannot, the discovery (through the contributions of Einstein, Planck, Bohr, Heisenberg and others) that the Newtonian principles are useless in atomic physics.

One who has been trained and conditioned to believe that readership studies based on direct interviews and opinion polls are reliable and valid, has difficulty accepting the discovery that they have been proved fallacious. Many research men still cannot accept the fact disclosed in recent years (through the contributions of Freud and others) that the traditional polling methods and readership study interviews do not reveal consumer behavior. These researchers cannot grasp the significance of the fact that consumers' verbalisms are not the same as their behavior. They still cannot believe that when a woman says she saw one ad (of a prestige establishment) and not the other (of a shop known for bargains) she is more likely to be expressing a wish than a fact.

Many women know that it is necessary to read certain ads to find out where they can buy for reasons of economy, but they are also aware that another store, out of their price range, has social status. Controlled studies reveal that responses in traditional direct-interview readership studies are frequently prompted by awareness of social status.

The consequences of the lack of a scientific marketing policy are best illustrated by two marketing events. One is of a food product. The other is not a food product, but it is sold in super markets.

In the case of the food product, controlled marketing research showed that the new package being considered was not as effective a marketing tool as the old one. The research showed clearly that the old package should be improved but that the radically changed package should not be adopted. Management chose to disregard the research findings and adopted the new package. The result was that sales dropped drastically and the old package had to be reinstated.

The other well-known product had a package change without the benefit of research. After the new package was out on the market a very short time, the company ran ads informing the public that it was reinstating the old package because many people objected to the new one. We conducted a study of the two packages (not for the company, but because we wanted to know the facts). The new package rated 14% in favorable associations, the old one 86%. A company that conducts marketing scientifically would have had such information before putting a new package on the market.

I was told that the executives now believe the old package is a "perfect" marketing tool. Our studies show that this is far from the truth. Actually, the package can be greatly improved.

The cost of controlled research is very small in comparison with the cost of coming out with a package that is weak as a marketing tool.

When I was a little boy, I was asked by my teacher to accompany him on a fishing trip. I did not think fishing was very exciting. My teacher motivated me to accompany him by telling me that he wanted me to make drawings of the fish he caught. "A fish has very lyrical form," he said. "What is the most important difference between a fish and a man?" I asked. "A man can think; a fish cannot," was his answer. I loved this teacher, but in the last forty years, I had numerous occasions to doubt this difference between a man and a fish.

LOUIS CHESKIN

Irving J. Lee and Laura L. Lee tell the following in their book, *Handling Barriers in Communication* (Harper & Brothers, 1958).

> Now, any of you who are fishermen know that min-
> nows are the natural food of the pike, so instead of being
> put into the same tank where the pike could eat the min-
> nows, they were separated by a glass partition. The pike
> could see the minnows all right, and he was hungry. He
> wasn't fed anything.
>
> Now, of course, the pike tried to get at the minnows.
> He kept smacking his nose up against the glass partition.
> He was hungry, and there was his food, but every time he
> tried to get at it he smacked his nose and got nothing. He
> did this hundreds of times before he gave up. But he did
> give up. He learned something. Even the nervous system
> of a fish can learn something. And what he learned was,
> 'Don't eat minnows.' His experience led to a new kind
> of behavior—a new evaluation, you might say. 'Don't eat
> minnows.'
>
> Now, at this point, the glass partition was removed.
>
> The minnows and the pike now swam about freely
> together, even bumping into each other. What do you
> suppose the pike's behavior was now? Do you think he
> tried to eat the minnows?
>
> Well, he didn't. He didn't touch them. The pike had
> learned a lesson. He had learned what he had learned!
> 'Don't eat minnows.' And the pike, surrounded by an
> abundance of his natural food, died of starvation. He
> knew what he knew. And he died with that knowledge."

How many men and women are just like the pike? No executive can behave like a pike and be successful in meeting new social
conditions and/or changed marketing situations.

CHAPTER 11

WHY IS RESEARCH SO VITAL IN PLANNING A NEW PRODUCT?

THE FOLLOWING appeared in *Printers' Ink* on September 5, 1958. "A. Stein & Co., New York manufacturer of Paris belts, suspenders and garters, is one organization that believes in coordinating all the elements of a marketing program.

The Stein management anticipated a highly competitive situation in their Paris belt line, in which impulse buying would play a still greater role than it did up to then. They, therefore, thought that the package should be improved, and evolved a specific concept for a package. They gave this packaging idea a name. They called it 'Vista-Dome.'

The company's marketing and advertising managers outlined the following specifications, after a great deal of research and investigation with retail dealers, for the 'Vista-Dome' package: a) ease of handling, b) easy to stack, c) effective in display, d) product protection, e) product enhancement and f) an image of quality—a belt that one would be proud to own and wear. This outline was turned over to the director of the design department.

The company had confidence in the 'Vista-Dome' theme and they liked what they saw being developed in product and in package design. But they wanted to be sure they were on the right track. After examining a number of well-known research sources and facilities, they decided to employ the services of Louis Cheskin and the Color Research Institute of Chicago.

There was enough information available about the product so that product testing was not needed. However, Cheskin proceeded first of all to have the Institute test the display effectiveness of several package designs that were submitted to him. The tests showed that one of the designs was very effective. However, one weak element was disclosed. After this was corrected, the revised package came through with high ratings in visibility, readability and eye-movement tests. It rated much higher than the competitive packages that were also put through the visual tests.

Then the package was put into a field test to discover people's associations with it. Sample packages were made up in two body colors and both were put into a field test of the association-type by Institute researchers. The controlled association test showed clearly that the *white* 'Vista-Dome' package had greater quality connotations and was the more effective marketing tool of the two.

As soon as the field test results on the package were disclosed, the advertising department began work on the ads and promotion material, and Associated Display Service was called in to design and produce new display racks. Packaging, product design, sales promotion and advertising can be handled in a coordinated program, if the planning is done under the guiding eye of research."

Then there was the problem of developing a sales aid. The company again showed originality in designing a sales aid that incorporated a report, with illustrations of the research, background information about Color Research Institute and illustrations of the package from various angles and the packages on the display racks.

Next was the planning of a sales personnel conference for launching the "Vista-Dome." In the sales conference as well as in the planning of the sales aid, A. Stein and Co. showed originality in using research not only for getting information but also as a selling aid. I was invited to be one of the speakers and was asked to cover three points in my talk: a) what are motivation research and unconscious-level testing and how does this type of research differ from the direct interviewing type of research; b) how was the "Vista-Dome" tested and what did the tests disclose; and c) why should belts be packaged, why not simply hang the belts on a rack?

Top management participated in the conference and inspired a feeling of high morale. The advertising manager and the account man from Cruttenden Advertising presented their programs. The following is my answer to the question, *Why Should Belts Be Packaged?*

The purely functional or practical purpose of a belt is to hold up a man's pants. However, if people bought belts only for this purpose, a man would buy two or three belts in a lifetime. Actually, a string or rope fulfills the practical need.

The average American man is not nearly as concerned with holding up his pants as he is about showing that he owns a beautiful belt, a rare belt, an unusual belt, or a costly belt.

Beauty, rarity, unusualness and costliness are "status" symbols. They are psychological factors. They are implements of his ego. They are vital elements of "prestige identification."

Nor does a woman buy a belt for her husband in order to keep his pants up. Every woman knows that a new belt will not be any more effective in keeping her husband's pants up than the old one.

When an American woman buys a belt for her man, she is motivated by psychological factors, not practical or functional.

She wants the belt because it has symbolic significance. Unconsciously, she chooses the type and quality of belt that represents her image of her man. One woman chooses a soft, chamois belt for her man. Another woman buys an elastic, slick, cowhide strap. A third prefers a rough surfaced, hard, alligator leather. Each type of belt has its character and personality, which the woman unconsciously matches to the personality and character of her husband.

In our highly industrialized complex society, in an economy of abundance, buying a belt is not a mere routine act, as it is in a craft society of low production and consumption sufficient for survival. In our atomic age, the mere act of buying a belt for your husband (or for yourself) is filled with deep psychological implications.

Marketing tests and experience have shown that normally a woman will not be attracted by belts hanging from a rack. Hanging belts do not arouse a woman's interest. A hanging belt has no attraction power. It is limp, unstimulating and undesirable. To the normal, healthy, energetic woman a hanging belt is not a symbol of virility or quality. It cannot possibly be associated with her man. It is not an appropriate symbol. It presents a negative image.

The manufacturer of belts who knows what the public wants and respects people's feelings puts the belts in attractive, psychologically meaningful packages.

In an appropriate package, a belt takes on a personality that it could not possibly have, hanging from a rack. An appropriate package reinforces the character of the belt. It protects the belt. It embellishes it. And it does still more, it gives the belt the psychologically meaningful effect of exclusiveness.

The fact that the belt is in a package means that it has not been handled by all sorts of people. The package symbolizes additional value, because normally, valuable objects are sold in attractive packages.

An appropriate package that is an effective marketing tool is no mere physical container. Such a package is endowed with great psychological significance. It is a positive image.

A belt that is encased in a psychologically potent package

symbolizes quality and therefore it easily becomes associated with deep affection or great love.

The belt that is housed and protected in a package that has favorable symbolism and psychologically potent color is found worthy of representing deep feelings and is naturally assigned the role of symbolizing respect, affection and even great love.

CHAPTER 12

EVOLVING A SYMBOL OF QUALITY

AT COLOR RESEARCH INSTITUTE where I deal with many clients, I have the opportunity to observe how companies, large and small, with diverse products, approach the problem of packaging and package changes.

I had to write an analysis of a test of a package design that had an 85% rating as a marketing tool. Writing this analysis was a pleasant task indeed. It is not often that I see a package design with 85% favorable associations.

In writing my conclusions of the field tests of the various designs for a new Parliament package, I reviewed the entire Parliament package testing procedure. I traced an approach to this packaging problem that is not often found in a packaging program.

The manner in which the Parliament executives approached the new package project reveals a practical, systematic procedure and a vital marketing philosophy.

Product quality was established before the problem of packaging was undertaken. After being assured of having a high quality product, by extensive laboratory and consumer testing, the Parliament executives approached the second most important problem, packaging.

The management of Parliament, Marlboro and Philip Morris cigarettes recognize that product quality is No. 1 in importance and the package becomes paramount after product quality has been assured. To them the package is a major marketing factor because it is the package that must visually symbolize and communicate to the public the high quality of the product.

I clearly remember the first meeting on Parliament I had with George Weissman, Hugh Cullman and Jet Lincoln. At this meeting I was told by them that they were ready to employ a top-notch designer or perhaps two designers on a new package for Parliament cigarettes. The purpose of the meeting was to form an outline of objectives.

At this meeting, we all agreed that the first objective was to find an effective brand-identifying image for the brand. A designer was to be assigned to develop a new symbol for Parliament. He was to design as many symbols as he could conceive that would express high quality and distinctive character. The brand-identifying image for Parliament cigarettes had to have high preference, that is, great appeal and easy memory retention.

The second step was for the designer to integrate the image into a package design. He was to produce a number of graphic arrangements or designs. On each package the brand-identifying image was to play the major role.

The third step was for the designer to produce each package design, or surface pattern, in a number of color plans.

After these three objectives for the designer were outlined, we began formulating a plan for testing the images and packages.

The first step was for Color Research Institute to provide the designer with several high preference colors.

These were to be chosen on the basis of tests that have been conducted by us during the last twenty years.

The second step was to test in the field, by means of controlled association tests conducted with 1200 smokers, a number of brand-identifying image designs created by the designer. This test would show which image receives the greatest number of favorable associations. It would specify which image symbolizes high quality and distinctive character. The image that rates the highest would be incorporated by the designer into a number of package designs.

The third step was to test a number of package designs by means of ocular measurements. Each design was to be submitted to a visibility test, a brand-name readability test and an eye-movement test that would show how the eyes travel over the package, whether the package holds attention. The ocular measurements would reveal consumers' involuntary reactions. They would show the display effectiveness of the package.

The fourth step was to take the package designs that received favorable ocular measurements and put each of them into association tests with from 600 to 1200 consumers. These association tests were to show the psychological effect each package as a whole had on the consumer. They were to be the same type that were used in the second step for evolving the brand-identifying image.

A subtle difference showed up between two packages. The association tests were not conclusive about which of the two packages was the more effective. This problem was solved by a sensation-transference test.

This test showed that one package symbolized the high quality of the product much better than the other package. The respondents in the test believed that the cigarettes in one package were of higher quality than those in the other package. It was the final Color Research Institute test. The next step was in a test market.

The most important aspect about everything I have said so far is that the program of developing a new package for Parliament cigarettes was systematic. It was planned, organized and had direction. Definite objectives were outlined for the designer and a specific procedure was set for the research to be conducted. Hugh Cullman, at that time the Brand Manager, and Jet Lincoln, Assistant Brand Manager, when we worked on this problem, studied every Color Research Institute report and consulted with Vice President in charge of Marketing, George Weissman and his

Planning Committee. The results of each test were passed on to the designer so that he could be guided by the information in each step of the development of the package.

Assuming that all other marketing factors were to be normal, or as usual, the new package for Parliament cigarettes could be expected to bring a great increase in sales. I could see that Parliament cigarettes in the new package would become a great success because our tests showed that the package was a very effective marketing tool. It is one of the few packages we ever had that came up with a rating of 85 in a field test.

A package that gets 70% favorable consumer attitudes (when it is tested by itself) is considered an effective marketing tool. One having between 75 % and 80% favorable associations is a very good marketing tool. A design or package that receives between 80% and 85% favorable associations is excellent. The box, wrapper or label with 85% favorable associations is superior.

Because our field tests are conducted on an unconscious level so that people react spontaneously to the object or package being tested, we wondered what people would say about this new Parliament cigarette package if they had a chance to express themselves verbally.

We used the new Parliament package as a control, as a means of getting people interested in another test. In control tests people are given a chance to say anything they please about the design or package that is used (as a control) to get the interest and participation of the subjects.

What smokers had to say about the new Parliament package revealed significant psychological aspects of packaging design.

One man, a carpenter, said that only an expensive cigarette could have such a package.

"What is there about this package that makes you say this?" he was asked. He couldn't say what specifically made him think it was an expensive brand, but he was sure it was. When he was told that Parliament cigarettes no longer were expensive, he showed surprise and said, "By the looks of the package I thought it costs twice as much as ordinary cigarettes."

A housewife remarked that the new Parliament cigarette package was "elegant." "What do you mean by elegant?" she was asked. "Refined and beautiful," she said and added, "of course it's Parliaments."

A secretary to a sales executive said, "The package is distinctive." She was asked what else she could say about the package and she said, "All I can say is that it is distinctive." She couldn't or wouldn't elaborate.

A man employed in a bank said "the package is regal," a stenographer said "it is neat," an auto mechanic said "it is quality" and a car salesman said "the package looks class." A housewife remarked that the package was "dignified" and a young factory worker said the package was "dandy." An insurance executive said the package was "distinguished" and a young girl in his office said it was "dignified."

One young lady said "the package is refined," another young lady thought it "swell" and a third young woman said "it is high fashion."

An executive of a machine manufacturing company said "the package is interesting." His secretary said it was "intriguing." Two stenographers said the package was "streamlined."

A few, very few, housewives said they liked the package because it had a "linen finish." Other housewives liked it because they liked blue. Some said they liked the embossed name. Others liked the gold.

Of 200 men and 200 women, only 35 men and 92 women gave specific but different reasons for liking the package. The others either wouldn't or couldn't give any reason for liking it. Yet they nearly all liked it.

Of 400 individuals only 15 (9 women and 6 men) mentioned the crest and chevron.

Controlled association-type tests conducted on an unconscious level with the Chevron-Crest image itself, independent of the package, showed the Chevron-Crest image received 92% favorable associations.

When people were given a chance to talk about the package with the Chevron-Crest, most of them said nothing about the Chevron-Crest, yet it is the dominant element on the package. What are the underlying psychological reasons for this? Why didn't most of the men and women who were interviewed say anything about the Chevron-Crest? Many of them talked freely about the blue color. Many did not hesitate to give the embossing and the gold as reasons for the package having appeal to them.

There is only one explanation why most of them said nothing about the Chevron-Crest image. It is that most people do not wish to admit to anyone, often not even to themselves, that they are influenced by or affected by a crest.

People like to give the impression of being practical. Some think it is normal and socially acceptable to like gold and even linen.

But a crest has no practical or material value. Deep in the subconscious the crest symbolizes luxury, nobility, royalty, prestige and high quality. Consciously, the crest stands for nothing practical. Nor is it commonly recognized in America as having aesthetic quality.

People will not say anything about the Chevron-Crest or about any other crest because they are not conscious that they are influenced by it or they feel that to admit that they are affected by a crest does not put them in a favorable light.

For one to say that he likes the Parliament package because of the Chevron-Crest, means that he has to say he is being influenced by the symbol of quality and prestige, not by the quality of the product itself.

Expressing appreciation of an abstract package design can be done openly and freely because the respondent considers the design independent of the contents. A color can be enjoyed for itself, independent of the object with which it is associated. Gold is commonly appreciated for its own value. Linen has no specific connotations of royalty or nobility and does have some practical connotations.

A crest, however, has no value in itself. It is a symbol, first and last, of royalty and nobility, of quality and prestige. People in America are greatly influenced by such symbols but they cannot or will not give them open recognition. They can talk about and are willing to talk about only things they consider practical.

That is why, in the controlled-association tests, the men and women reacted most favorably to the Chevron-Crest image but in the direct interviews people couldn't or wouldn't say that they were influenced by a crest. The tests that were conducted on an unconscious level show that the Chevron-Crest is the symbol of high quality, because in the association-type tests, the men and women reacted spontaneously and naturally and thus revealed their true or real attitudes.

In the direct interviews about the package the respondents wanted to find practical or common sense reasons. Few are willing to declare that they want to be regal or that they enjoy things that are regal. Yet unconsciously people do strive for such things. They do not wish to declare that they are interested in prestige. Yet they naturally desire prestige, usually unconsciously. Often consciously or deliberately they seek "status" and want to identify themselves with "status" symbols.

Normally, consumers like to think and are always willing to say that they are interested in the quality of the product. Consciously, they buy a brand because in their opinion it is a product of high quality.

However, Color Research Institute tests have repeatedly demonstrated that the product of high quality must have a high quality symbol. It is the symbol that signals to the consumer's unconscious mind that the product is of high quality. The consumer is not conscious of the effect that the symbol has on him.

Tea from one container tasted better than it did from another. Yet the tea was the same, only the containers differed. Canned vegetables from one can tasted much better to housewives than the vegetables from another can. Yet the only difference was that the labels on the cans were different. These are typical examples of sensation transference.

Few men or women are aware that they are influenced by a container, a label, a color or a crest. Because people are not aware of sensation transference, they cannot tell us about it.

Those who do say they like the design of a label or carton, think of the design as unrelated to the product itself. The typical housewife will not say that she is buying a brand of food, soap or cigarettes because she likes the package.

Few men will say that they buy their cars because of symbolism. They search for practical reasons to give for buying a certain make of car. The man who likes "good clothes" will give practical reasons for buying a certain brand. Usually, the real reasons are those of "status." The actual reasons are most likely to be "prestige identification" or "ego expression."

It does no good for an inferior product to have a high quality symbol. For a high quality product, symbolism of high quality is a "must" in successful marketing. Repeated sales depend on a combination of high quality product and high quality symbolism.

A high quality symbol is normally an unconscious factor to the consumer, but a high quality product is a conscious factor to the consumer.

Our tests show that the people know that the name, Parliament, stands for a high quality cigarette. The brand name itself is a symbol of quality.

The controlled-association tests of the new package show that men and women associate the package with high quality. The package consists of only two major design elements, the Chevron-Crest and the brand name, Parliament.

In other words, the Chevron-Crest is the natural companion

for the name, Parliament. It reinforces the high quality connotation of the name, Parliament.

The tests of the Chevron-Crest image by itself, and of the package as a whole, show clearly that the Chevron-Crest is a symbol of what people feel. They are deeply affected by it. But people feel that this symbol, like many emotionally-significant symbols, is not a subject for discussion.

CHAPTER 13

WHAT IS THERE IN A LOGO?

MANAGEMENT attitudes toward logotypes range from fanatical attachment to the original logo, to complete indifference to the logo. The two extremes have both amazed me and interested me. I find complete attachment to the original is mostly among company presidents. Generally, there is complete indifference among designers. I have known several company presidents and brand managers who would not change a hairline on the logo. And I have known presidents and brand managers who considered the logo as a mere typesetting or lettering problem.

Enlightened management knows that a logo is a vital part of the company or brand image. At the same time up-to-date managers know that concepts and tastes are gradually changing. They are aware that marketing conditions, competitive factors and display situations have changed considerably in recent years. Because of this awareness, realistic management periodically examines the logo as well as other vital marketing factors.

Before alert managers make any kind of marketing decision, they submit the problem to reliable marketing research. The following is the actual report, although in part, of how the executives of Nestlé proceeded with their examination of the logotype on the Nescafé label and of the label as a whole.

A top-notch designer was employed. He (Egmont Arens)

produced a number of designs which were sent to Color Research Institute for ocular measurements and for color and image ratings. Each of the new designs was superior in display effectiveness to the old label. They were more effective than the old label in all three ocular tests.

In my analysis, I pointed out that the logo on the old label had poor readability and that there were psychological factors involved. My first question was, "What will be the attitudes of consumers toward a change of the well-known Nescafé logo?" I recommended field testing three new logo designs created by the designer and the old logo, before proceeding any further with the label designs.

The new logo designs and the old logo were sent to us to be put into a field test with 800 consumers. Describing the logos will aid in understanding the test results. Design 1 was a completely new logo with no resemblance to the old one. Design 2 was the old logo. Designs 3 and 4 were modified forms of the old logo.

The test showed clearly that the consumers did not react favorably to the No. 1 logo, which was the completely new one. This design had more than twice as many unfavorable responses than favorable ones. To "experts" this logo was modern, to the consumers it was "least modern" of the four. (Tables I and II.)

The old logo did very well in favorable responses, in spite of the fact that it did poorly in the readability measurement. The number of associations the old logo had with "high quality" showed what consumers thought of the brand. Design 3 came out high in favorable associations and also came out best in readability measurements. Design 4 was almost as good.

The No. 3 modified logo was tested by itself. The test showed that it had 94% favorable associations, which is remarkable. A logo with 70% favorable associations (when tested by itself) is considered good. (Tables III and IV.)

Now management had information showing clearly that the old Nescafé logo had great meaning to the public. The test results revealed that the logo could be modified in order to increase readability, as in Design 3 or Design 4, but could not be completely changed without alienating the consumers. On the basis of this information, management decided to give the designer authorization to proceed with designing the labels, incorporating logo No. 3.

The designer produced a number of label designs, that differed in arrangement and in color, but not in logo. The designs were sent to us for ocular measurements and color ratings. Two of them came out with very high ratings in all three ocular tests—visibility, readability and eye-movement. The dominant color of one of these rated higher in preference and in favorable association with the product. (Table V.)

Management now made the decision to have us test the new label design against the old label and also to have the new design tested by itself. The results of the two tests are very revealing. (Tables VI, VII, VIII, IX and X.)

These tests provided a basis for management decision to go to market with the new label. The Nestlé Company executives followed a similar procedure in their examinations and revisions of the marketing aspects of their other products.

Report for THE NESTLÉ COMPANY, INC.
Date: January 25, 1957
Association Test: FOUR NESCAFÉ LOGO DESIGNS
Sample: 814 Consumers

TABLE I—Favorable and Unfavorable Associations
(Number and Per Cent)

	Design 1		Design 2 (old logo)		Design 3		Design 4	
Favorable	540	33%	835	55%	609	65%	643	59%
Unfavorable	1084	67%	695	45%	332	35%	443	41%
Total	1624	100%	1530	100%	941	100%	1086	100%

TABLE II—Number of Associations with Attitude Words

	Design 1	Design 2 (old logo)	Design 3	Design 4
Favorable				
high quality	155	307	222	177
clear (easy to read)	235	253	179	259
most attractive	150	275	208	207
Total	540	835	609	643
Unfavorable				
low quality	405	183	110	158
confusing (hard to read)	272	310	129	149
least attractive	407	202	93	136
Total	1084	695	332	443
Unclassified				
familiar	188	317	217	150
unfamiliar	405	246	163	191
most modern	84	357	197	204
least modern	538	124	69	77
Grand Total	2839	2574	1587	1708

ANALYSIS

Logo Design 1 received 33% favorable associations, Logo Design 2 received 55%, Logo Design 3 received 65% and Logo Design 4 received 59%. Logo Designs 2 and 3 were "familiar" and Designs 2, 3 and 4 were "most modem." There were no appreciable differences between men and women in the proportion of favorable responses to Logo Designs 2, 3 and 4.

Report for THE NESTLÉ COMPANY, INC.
Date: March 7, 1957
Association Test: NESCAFÉ LOGO (Design 3)
Sample: 841 Consumers

TABLE III—Favorable and Unfavorable Associations
(Number and Per Cent)

616 Women

	Number	Per Cent
Favorable	2747	93%
Unfavorable	200	7%
Total	2947	100%

225 Men

	Number	Per Cent
Favorable	1050	96%
Unfavorable	47	4%
Total	1097	100%

841 Consumers

	Number	Per Cent
Favorable	3797	94%
Unfavorable	247	6%
Total	4044	100%

TABLE IV—Number of Associations with Attitude Words

	616 Women	225 Men	841 Total
Favorable			
familiar	598	223	821
good	582	216	798
high quality	534	208	742
superior	508	208	716
for me	525	195	720
Total	2747	1050	3797
Unfavorable			
unfamiliar	16	4	20
bad	24	4	28
low quality	62	11	73
inferior	35	8	43
not for me	63	20	83
Total	200	47	247
Unclassified			
distinctive	327	126	453
ordinary	254	96	350
Grand Total	3528	1319	4847

ANALYSIS

In this test the Nescafé Logo has 94% favorable associations. This is a very large proportion of favorable responses. We seldom have figures this high. The Logo is amazingly high in association with "familiar" and "high quality."

Note that "distinctive" does not come up very high. This was due to the fact that the Logo was "familiar" and to many people familiar objects are not distinctive.

Report for THE NESTLÉ COMPANY, INC.
Date: March 29, 1957
Subject: NESCAFÉ INSTANT COFFEE LABEL (New Design)

TABLE V—Ocular Measurements of New Design

Tests		Ratings
Visibility	—	88
Readability	—NESCAFÉ	89
	—COFFEE	87
Eye-movement	—Eyes fell on NESCAFÉ, moved to *Instant,* to COFFEE and left package. Attention was held at each point.	A (Excellent)

ANALYSIS

The visibility is very good.

The readability is very good.

The eye-flow and attention-holding are excellent.

The involuntary reactions to this label design are very good indeed.

RECOMMENDATIONS

I recommend that we put this label into a field test of the association type. It is advisable to test it by itself and against the present label.

Report for THE NESTLÉ COMPANY, INC.
Date: April 24, 1957
Association Tests: NESCAFÉ LABELS
Test A: New Gold Foil Design—*Sample:* 403 Consumers
Test B: Old Label vs. New Gold Foil Design—*Sample:* 400 Consumers

**TABLE VI—Test A: Favorable and Unfavorable Associations
(Number and Per Cent)**

	Number	Per Cent
Favorable	2289	79%
Unfavorable	620	21%
Total	2909	100%

TABLE VII—Test A: Number of Associations with Attitude Words

Favorable	New Design
good	304
high quality	295
expensive	268
superior	292
attractive	271
appealing	296
desirable	283
for me *	280
Total	2289
Unfavorable	
bad	67
low quality	66
cheap	84
inferior	67
unattractive	88
unappealing	77
undesirable	73
not for me	98
Total	620
Unclassified	
distinctive	214
ordinary	143
modern	276
old-fashioned	107
Grand Total	3649

* Preference

TABLE VIII—Test B: Favorable and Unfavorable Associations (Number and Per Cent)

	Present Label		New Design	
Favorable	1009	33%	2188	69%
Unfavorable	2081	67%	964	31%
Total	3090	100%	3152	100%

TABLE IX—Test B: Number of Associations with Attitude Words

Favorable	Present Label	New Design
good	137	268
high quality	130	273
expensive	115	275
superior	122	273
attractive	127	276
appealing	127	275
desirable	127	275
for me *	124	273
Total	1009	2188
Unfavorable		
bad	247	126
low quality	255	119
cheap	265	117
inferior	262	117
unattractive	263	114
unappealing	265	120
undesirable	259	126
not for me	265	125
Total	2081	964
Unclassified		
distinctive	108	292
ordinary	286	102
modern	109	283
old-fashioned	278	106
Grand Total	3871	3935

* Preference

LOUIS CHESKIN

TABLE X—Test B: Attitudes Ranked

Ranks	Present Label		Ranks	New Design	
(1)	ordinary	286	(1)	distinctive	292
(2)	old-fashioned	278	(2)	modern	283
(3)	cheap	265	(3)	attractive	276
(4)	unappealing	265	(4)	expensive	275
(5)	not for me	265	(5)	appealing	275
(6)	unattractive	263	(6)	desirable	275
(7)	inferior	262	(7)	high quality	273
(8)	undesirable	259	(8)	superior	273
(9)	low quality	255	(9)	for me	273
(10)	bad	247	(10)	good	268
(11)	good	137	(11)	bad	126
(12)	high quality	130	(12)	undesirable	126
(13)	attractive	127	(13)	not for me	125
(14)	appealing	127	(14)	unappealing	120
(15)	desirable	127	(15)	low quality	119
(16)	for me	124	(16)	cheap	117
(17)	superior	122	(17)	inferior	117
(18)	expensive	115	(18)	unattractive	114
(19)	modern	109	(19)	old-fashioned	106
(20)	distinctive	108	(20)	ordinary	102

ANALYSIS

In Test A the New Gold Foil Design receives 79% favorable associations. It has the largest number of associations with "good," "appealing" and "high quality."

In Test B the new design receives 69% favorable associations and the Present Label 33%. The new design is consistently high in association with all the favorable attitude words.

Test B shows clearly that the new label is more than twice as effective as the old label.

Note that when the new design is tested by itself it has 10% more effectiveness than in the test against the Present Label.

CHAPTER 14

HOW IMPORTANT IS AN OLD SYMBOL?

PACKAGING has grown to the proportions of a giant industry. Every alert marketing executive has in recent years become conscious of packaging. Management is generally aware that the package is an important marketing factor. Progressive management is examining the packaging aspects of its business in a new light.

The management of Hawley & Hoops was looking into the packaging of Uncle Ben's Rice in the summer of 1956. Color Research Institute was employed to get the following information about Uncle Ben's Rice.

1. Is Uncle Ben's trademark of value in marketing?
   a) What value does the symbol have in the South?
   b) What value does the symbol have in the North?

2. Is the "appetite-appeal" illustration of any marketing value?

The test of the trademark (portrait of Uncle Ben) without the package showed that in the South the image had 80% favorable associations, and 82% associated the image with Uncle Ben's and 10% with Ben's. In the North the image had 76% favorable associations, and 81% associated the trademark with Uncle Ben's and 7% with Ben's. Management could see that this old trademark had great brand-identity and rated remarkably high in favorable consumer attitudes. (Tables XI and XII.)

The second test was of a new package design, "a modern, up-to-date, clean looking package design," against the old Uncle Ben's Rice package with the food illustration. The test showed that in the South the old package had 94% favorable associations and the new design, without food illustration, received 5% favorable associations. In the North the old package rated 92% and the new one 7%. (Tables XIII, XIV, XV, and XVI.)

The two tests showed clearly that Hawley & Hoops had a valuable property in the Uncle Ben's symbol and that the "appetite appeal" illustration was a great asset indeed. These are among the most remarkable test results of an old brand symbol and an old package versus a new one that we have seen at Color Research Institute.

Having obtained this information, management ordered new package designs with instructions to the designer that the old trademark and a new, improved "appetite appeal" illustration must be components of the package.

Five new designs were submitted to ocular measurements. The ratings showed that they all were high in display effectiveness, but that the yellow packages had greater visibility from the shelf than the white ones.

Because white and yellow are psychological factors as well as display-attraction elements, I recommended a field test.

This study shows clearly that the basic elements of the old package had meaning to consumers and that the package had to be improved in marketing effectiveness without changing its identity.

Report for HAWLEY & HOOPS, INC.
Date: August 3, 1956
Association Test: UNCLE BEN'S TRADEMARK
             Trademark Image without Brand Identity
Sample: 402 Women

**TABLE XI—Favorable and Unfavorable Associations
(Number and Per Cent)**

Sample: 200 Women		Area: South
	Number	Per Cent
Favorable	477	80%
Unfavorable	123	20%
Total	600	100%
Sample: 202 Women		Area: North
	Number	Per Cent
Favorable	461	76%
Unfavorable	143	24%
Total	604	100%

TABLE XII—Attitudes Ranked

	200 Women—South			202 Women—North	
(1)	good	189	(1)	good	175
(2)	high quality	181	(2)	high quality	172
(3)	expensive	107	(3)	expensive	114
(4)	cheap	93	(4)	cheap	86
(5)	low quality	19	(5)	low quality	30
(6)	bad	11	(6)	bad	27

ANALYSIS

In the South the trademark had 80% favorable associations.

Out of a sampling of 200 women, 189 associated the trademark with "good," 181 with "high quality," 107 with "expensive," 93 with "cheap." Only 19 individuals associated the trademark with "low quality" and only 11 individuals associated it with "bad."

Eighty-two-per cent associated the trademark with Uncle Ben's and 10% with Ben's. (Table not shown.)

In the North the trademark had 76% favorable associations.

Out of a sampling of 202 women, 175 associated the trademark with "good" and 172 with "high quality."

Eighty-one per cent associated the trademark with Uncle Ben's and 7% with Ben's. (Table not shown.)

This test shows that consumers' attitudes toward the trademark are highly favorable and that the identity of the trademark is great.

Report for HAWLEY & HOOPS, INC.
Date: August 3, 1956
Association Test: UNCLE BEN'S RICE CARTONS
New Design (without illustration)
vs.
Present Package (with illustration)
Sample: 601 Women

TABLE XIII—Favorable and Unfavorable Associations
(Number and Per Cent)

Sample: 300 Women		Area: South
	New Design	Present Package
Favorable	127	2272
Unfavorable	2268	136
Total	2395	2408
	New Design	Present Package
Favorable	5%	94%
Unfavorable	95%	6%
Total	100%	100%

TABLE XIV—Attitudes Ranked

Sample: 300 Women   *Area:* South

Ranks	New Design		Ranks	Present Package	
(1)	unappetizing	290	(1)	appetizing	291
(2)	unappealing	288	(2)	good	289
(3)	bad	287	(3)	appealing	287
(4)	undesirable	287	(4)	desirable	286
(5)	low quality	286	(5)	for me	286
(6)	not for me	286	(6)	high quality	282
(7)	cheap	276	(7)	distinctive	278
(8)	commonplace	268	(8)	expensive	273
(9)	expensive	27	(9)	cheap	34
(10)	distinctive	21	(10)	commonplace	30
(11)	high quality	18	(11)	low quality	14
(12)	desirable	14	(12)	not for me	14
(13)	for me	14	(13)	undesirable	13
(14)	appealing	13	(14)	unappealing	12
(15)	good	11	(15)	bad	11
(16)	appetizing	9	(16)	unappetizing	8

TABLE XV—Favorable and Unfavorable Associations
(Number and Per Cent)

Sample: 301 Women   *Area:* North

	New Design	Present Package
Favorable	167	2240
Unfavorable	2211	195
Total	2378	2435
	New Design	Present Package
Favorable	7%	92%
Unfavorable	93%	8%
Total	100%	100%

LOUIS CHESKIN

TABLE XVI—Attitudes Ranked

Sample: 301 Women			Area: North		
Ranks	New Design		Ranks	Present Package	
(1)	unappetizing	285	(1)	appetizing	288
(2)	undesirable	284	(2)	appealing	284
(3)	unappealing	283	(3)	desirable	282
(4)	not for me	282	(4)	for me	282
(5)	low quality	278	(5)	good	277
(6)	cheap	278	(6)	high quality	276
(7)	bad	277	(7)	distinctive	276
(8)	commonplace	244	(8)	expensive	275
(9)	expensive	26	(9)	commonplace	57
(10)	high quality	25	(10)	bad	24
(11)	good	24	(11)	low quality	23
(12)	distinctive	24	(12)	cheap	22
(13)	desirable	19	(13)	not for me	19
(14)	for me	19	(14)	unappealing	18
(15)	appealing	17	(15)	unappetizing	16
(16)	appetizing	13	(16)	undesirable	16

ANALYSIS

In the South the new design had 5% favorable associations and the old carton 94%. In the North the new design had 7% favorable associations and the old carton 92%.

This test shows conclusively that the present package is a much more effective marketing tool than the new design.

Report for HAWLEY & HOOPS, INC.
Date: August 23, 1956
Subject: NEW UNCLE BEN'S RICE CARTON AND BAG DESIGNS

Design 1:5—"Uncle Ben's Rice" on One Line, White Background
Design 2:5—"Uncle Ben's Rice" on Two Lines, White Background
Design 3:5—"Uncle Ben's Rice" on One Line, Yellow Background

Design 4:5—"Uncle Ben's Rice" on Two Lines, Yellow Background
Design 5:5—"Uncle Ben's Rice" Carton Design

ANALYSIS

Ocular Measurements (Statistics not shown)

The carton design (5:5) is optically very effective, yet the identity of the old package remains.

The visibility from the shelf is excellent.

The readability of *Uncle Ben's* is very good. *Rice* is excellent in readability.

The eyes travel smoothly over the front panel and attention is held.

The designs for bags are all very effective optically.

All four are excellent in eye-movement, that is, each of them guides the eyes smoothly and holds attention.

The two yellow packages have much greater visibility from the shelf than the white packages. The yellow ones are excellent, the white ones good.

There is little difference in readability between *Uncle Ben's Rice* in one line and *Uncle Ben's* in one line and *Rice* below. Both are very good.

The visibility superiority of the yellow bag design is a display advantage. However, before assuming that the yellow is a marketing advantage, we must test to determine whether a yellow bag or a white bag is associated with "high quality" and other favorable attributes.

It is also vital to find out whether a bag or a box is the more effective marketing tool.

We should now conduct the following two tests, both of the association-type, to find out consumer attitudes.

> *Test 1*—Yellow bag design against white bag design
> *Test 2*—Yellow bag design against yellow box design

These tests will reveal quality associations, price associations and other favorable and/or unfavorable consumer attitudes.

CHAPTER 15

IMPROVING THE TASTE WITHOUT CHANGING THE INGREDIENTS

W. B. DONER & COMPANY is a very creative agency. I have seen some very interesting ideas come out of their offices. The study we conducted of the campaign for The National Brewing Company showed that the theme "It's Brewed on the Shores of Chesapeake Bay" is one of the most effective commercials ever tested by Color Research Institute.

Julian Grace, W. B. Doner partner, and account executive for Faygo, a well-known soft drink in Detroit, said to me, "We have a client who manufactures a beverage of the highest quality. How can you improve the taste without changing the ingredients? I was told that you can do it."

I told him that it could be done with a label design. He smiled and said that he knew that and already had discussed the matter with a designer and wanted my help. I outlined the procedure to him.

In about two weeks several label designs arrived for ocular measurements and color ratings. Two of the designs came out very well in the tests. I recommended putting more accent on the brand-identifying image and a slight change in the logo, to improve readability. I also prescribed a color of higher preference than the one used by the designer.

When the revised design was put through ocular measurements (Table XVII), it proved to rate high in display effectiveness and we proceeded to go into field tests with the new design by itself and the new design against the old label.

The results shown here in part reveal that the new design, when tested by itself, came out with 79% favorable associations. (Tables XX and XXI.) When tested against the old label, the new design received 65% favorable associations and the old label (Tables XVIII and XIX.)

It is vital to keep in mind that in the actual testing procedure, the word label is not used. We are testing products, not labels. Consciously, consumers do not consider labels of any consequence.

Since Julian Grace wanted to know whether the taste could be improved by changing the label, we conducted a taste test, in which sensation transference was involved. (Tables XXII, XXIII, and XXIV.)

The report shows that 60% found that the orange soda from the bottle with the new label tasted better than the orange soda from the bottle with the old label. Of course, actually there was no difference between the two.

An interesting picture of semantic contrasts appears in Table XXIV. Note that "higher price," and "better quality" and "better flavor" are at the top with the new design. "Lower price," "poorer quality" and "poorer flavor" are at the top with the old label.

The new label design has become the symbol for the entire company. It appears on shipping cases, letterheads, signs, trucks, and of course, it is used in all ads and filmed commercials. The label is a device for upgrading the corporate brand image as well as the package itself.

Report for W. B. DONER & COMPANY
Date: April 17, 1957
Subject: FAYGO ORANGE SODA (New Design)

TABLE XVII—Ocular Measurements—Label and Neckband

Test		Ratings
Visibility	—	90
Readability	—FAYGO	87
Eye-movement	—Eyes fell on gold foil at top of bottle, moved to neck band, dropped to shield with *F*, moved to *FAYGO* to *ORANGE SODA* and left label. Attention was held at each point.	A (Excellent)

ANALYSIS

The visibility of the label is excellent

The brand name readability is very good.

The eye-flow and attention-holding are excellent.

Report for W. B. DONER & COMPANY

Date: September 12, 1957

Association Test: PRESENT FAYGO LABEL vs. NEW FAYGO DESIGN

Sample: 205 Consumers

**TABLE XVIII—Favorable and Unfavorable Associations
(Number and Per Cent)**

	Present Label	New Design
Favorable	436	796
Unfavorable	792	436
Total	1228	1232
	Present Label	New Design
Favorable	36%	65%
Unfavorable	64%	35%
Total	100%	100%

TABLE XIX—Number of Associations with Attitude Words

	Present Label	New Design
Favorable		
good	50	157
high quality	75	131
more expensive	92	113
superior	78	127
more attractive	69	135
for me	72	133
Total	436	796
Unfavorable		
bad	155	49
low quality	133	72
less expensive	112	93
inferior	127	78
less attractive	132	73
not for me	133	71
Total	792	436
Grand Total	1228	1232

Report for W. B. DONER & COMPANY
Date: September 12, 1957
Association Test: NEW FAYGO DESIGN (Orange Soda)
Sample: 204 Consumers

**TABLE XX—Favorable and Unfavorable Associations
(Number and Per Cent)**

	Number	Per Cent
Favorable	973	79%
Unfavorable	256	21%
Total	1229	100%

TABLE-XXI—Number of Associations with Attitude Words

Favorable	New Design
good	189
expensive	110
attractive	178
high quality	169
superior	171
for me	156
Total	973
Unfavorable	
bad	15
inexpensive	95
unattractive	28
low quality	35
inferior	34
not for me	49
Total	256
Grand Total	1229

Report for W. B. DONER & COMPANY

Date: September 18, 1957

Sensation Transference Test: FAYGO LABEL vs. NEW DESIGN

Sample: 220 Consumers

TABLE XXII—Favorable and Unfavorable Associations (Number and Per Cent)

	Present Label	New Design
Favorable	259	395
Unfavorable	392	260
Total	651	655
	Present Label	New Design
Favorable	40%	60%
Unfavorable	60%	40%
Total	100%	100%

TABLE XXIII—Number of Associations with Attitude Words

	Present Label	New Design
Favorable		
better quality	89	131
higher price	80	133
better flavor	90	131
Total	259	395
Unfavorable		
poorer quality	129	91
lower price	134	81
poorer flavor	129	88
Total	392	260
Unclassified		
too much carbonation	83	59
carbonation just right	87	126
not enough carbonation	52	43
Grand Total	873	883

TABLE XXIV—Attitudes Ranked

Ranks Present Label		Ranks New Design	
(1) lower price	134	(1) higher price	133
(2) poorer quality	129	(2) better quality	131
(3) poorer flavor	129	(3) better flavor	131
(4) better flavor	90	(4) carbonation just right	126
(5) better quality	89	(5) poorer quality	91
(6) carbonation just right	87	(6) poorer flavor	88
(7) too much carbonation	83	(7) lower price	81
(8) higher price	80	(8) too much carbonation	59
(9) not enough carbonation	52	(9) not enough carbonation	43

CHAPTER 16

WHAT'S IN A NAME?

THE PRESIDENT of Plenty Products, Inc. came to discuss the packaging of a new product, a high quality dessert, which he called Plentifors.

I pointed out to Mr. H. B. Burt that the name "Plentifors" has a quantitative connotation not one of quality. "This product needs a name that has quality connotations."

I recommended testing a number of names. In about a week Mr. Burt came up with four names.

The four newly proposed names and "Plentifors" were put into a controlled association test with 800 potential consumers, in four parts of the country. As in other tests conducted by Color Research Institute, this was integrated with a control test. We did not ask the respondents to judge names. There was no mention of names in the test. The purpose of the actual test was not told to the respondents. The testing procedure was indirect. (Tables XXV, XXVI, and XXVII.)

Part of the report, showing the test results of the entire sample of consumers, is shown here. There was no significant difference in results between the four areas. (Names for other products often come out favorably in some areas and unfavorably in others.)

This test provided a basis for management decision in choosing a name with maximum marketing effectiveness.

Report for PLENTY PRODUCTS, INC.

Date: October 11, 1957

Association Test: FIVE ICE CREAM DESSERT NAMES

Sample: 806 Consumers

TABLE XXV—Price Associations

Price	(Per Package of Four Individual Desserts)				
	Fancifors	Plentifors	Splendors	Celestials	Angelfors
79¢	129	46	164	205	257
69¢	109	116	175	187	221
59¢	139	142	225	189	106
49¢	245	159	159	123	100
39¢	160	354	68	97	113

TABLE XXVI—Favorable and Unfavorable Associations
(Number and Per Cent)

	Number				
	Fanci-fors	Plenti-fors	Splen-dors	Celes-tials	Angel-fors
Favorable	590	333	1206	998	1677
Unfavorable	1015	2140	348	767	510
Total	1605	2473	1554	1765	2187
	Per Cent				
	Fanci-fors	Plenti-fors	Splen-dors	Celes-tials	Angel-fors
Favorable	37%	13%	78%	57%	77%
Unfavorable	63%	87%	22%	43%	23%
Total	100%	100%	100%	100%	100%

TABLE XXVII—Number of Associations with Attitude Words

Favorable	Fanci-fors	Plenti-fors	Splen-dors	Celes-tials	Angel-fors
good	94	67	236	128	282
highest quality	96	59	209	207	228
most expensive	145	52	186	197	217
most desirable	79	55	188	173	308
most appetizing	92	49	178	135	340
for me *	84	51	209	158	302
Total	590	333	1206	998	1677
Unfavorable					
bad	189	322	50	159	86
lowest quality	159	394	67	99	73
least expensive	156	392	64	84	90
least desirable	162	358	48	134	93
least appetizing	169	359	57	135	75
not for me	180	315	62	156	93
Total	1015	2140	348	767	510
Unclassified					
special	101	37	187	206	270
ordinary	122	445	109	66	58
fancy	209	25	130	202	240
plain	97	453	126	67	62
Grand Total	2134	3433	2106	2306	2817

* Preference

ANALYSIS

SPLENDORS received 78% favorable associations.

ANGELFORS received 77% favorable associations.

In the price association part of the test, both SPLENDORS and ANGELFORS have greater associations with 59¢ and above, than with the prices below 59¢.

The test clearly shows that both the name SPLENDORS and the name ANGELFORS are effective marketing tools. The other three names have no marketing effectiveness.

CHAPTER 17

HOW IMPORTANT IS A TRADEMARK?

ARNOLD NIEMEYER, President of Arnold M. Niemeyer and Associates, an ad agency in St. Paul, Minnesota, came to discuss the marketing of Pearson's Candy. He brought the line of packages and told me that the product was of the highest quality.

My first response to the packages was that they lacked a brand-identifying image. Niemeyer agreed. "How are they in display effectiveness?" he asked. This I could not tell without ocular measurements. Niemeyer and I proceeded to pick out two packages to be put through ocular measurements.

In the report on the two packages, I interpreted the meaning of the visibility, readability and eye-movement ratings. I pointed out the weak elements and the strong ones in the packages, as they were revealed in the test ratings and brought up the lack of a brand-identifying image. I recommended that a brand-identifying image should be developed before doing anything about the packages.

Arnold Niemeyer and the President of Pearson's Candy employed a designer to create a trademark that would be put on every package in the Pearson's Candy line. The designer was provided by us with some basic images and colors that rated high in preference, retention in the memory and in favorable associations.

The designer produced three image designs. They were put through ocular measurements and each came out favorably. The designs were therefore put into the field for testing consumers' attitudes. First the designs were tested in pairs. (Tables XXVIII, XXIX, and XXX.) Finally, the design that came out best in the paired comparative tests was tested by itself. (Tables XXXI and XXXII.)

My analysis and part of the report is shown here. This study reveals a fact that is difficult for many brand managers to accept. Most executives still look for rational answers to marketing problems. It is not within the experience of a brand manager to see an apparently minor difference in the design of a trademark as a major factor in the consumer attitudes toward the product of which the trademark is the symbol.

Note that in Test A the only difference between the two designs is the position of the crown. Yet one design received 82% favorable associations and the other received only 19% favorable associations (Table XXVIII). The other tests in this series also reveal how minor details can be major factors.

Here is evidence that brand symbols or brand-identifying designs play major roles in marketing and that design details are vital factors in the success or failure of a marketing program.

This report shows it is dangerous to assume that all crowns, crests and other symbolic images are equally effective as marketing devices. The character of the image plays a vital role.

Report for ARNOLD M. NIEMEYER & ASSOCIATES
Date: October 18, 1957
Association Tests: PEARSON'S CANDY TRADEMARKS
TEST A: Black and White Trademarks (200 Consumers)
Crown in Open vs. Crown Inset
TEST B: Red and Gold Trademarks (200 Consumers)
Crown in Open vs. Crown Inset
TEST C: Black and White Trademarks (201 Consumers)
Crown in Open vs. Crown Inset {Gray)
TEST D: Red and Gold Trademarks (200 Consumers)
Crown in Open (.Revised) vs. Crown Inset
TEST E: Red and Gold Trademark (209 Consumers)
Crown in Open {Revised)

TABLE XXVIII—TEST A: Favorable and Unfavorable Associations
(Number and Per Cent)

	Crown Open		Crown Inset	
Favorable	977	82%	222	19%
Unfavorable	218	18%	976	81%
Total	1195	100%	1198	100%

TABLE XXIX—TEST A: Attitudes Ranked

Ranks	Crown Open		Ranks	Crown Inset	
(1)	good	167	(1)	bad	167
(2)	high quality	164	(2)	low quality	164
(3)	for me	164	(3)	less attractive	164
(4)	more attractive	164	(4)	not for me	163
(5)	superior	162	(5)	inferior	162
(6)	more expensive	156	(6)	less expensive	156
(7)	less expensive	39	(7)	more expensive	43
(8)	inferior	38	(8)	superior	38
(9)	not for me	36	(9)	for me	36
(10)	low quality	36	(10)	high quality	36
(11)	less attractive	36	(11)	more attractive	36
(12)	bad	33	(12)	good	33

TABLE XXX—TEST A: Number of Associations with Attitude Words

	Crown in Open	Crown Inset
Favorable		
good	167	33
high quality	164	36
more expensive	156	43
more attractive	164	36
superior	162	38
for me	164	36
Total	977	222
Unfavorable		
bad	33	167
low quality	36	164
less expensive	39	156
less attractive	36	164
inferior	38	162
not for me	36	163
Total	218	976
Grand Total	1195	1198

TABLE XXXI—TEST E: Favorable and Unfavorable Associations (Number and Per Cent)

Crown in Open (Revised)	
	Number
Favorable	1034
Unfavorable	110
Total	1144
	Per Cent
Favorable	90%
Unfavorable	10%
Total	100%

TABLE XXXII—TEST E: Number of Associations with Attitude Words

	Crown in Open (Revised)
Favorable	
good	197
high quality	181
expensive	135
attractive	188
superior	174
for me	159
Total	1034
Unfavorable	
bad	2
low quality	11
inexpensive	65
unattractive	6
inferior	7
not for me	19
Total	110
Grand Total	1144

ANALYSIS

In Test A (black and white trademarks), the Crown in Open has 82% favorable associations. The Crown Inset has 19% favorable associations.

In Test B (red and gold trademarks), the Crown Inset has 73% favorable associations. The Crown in Open has 27% favorable associations (statistics not shown).

These two tests show that the Crown in Open is effective in black and white but not in red and gold. The Crown Inset is effective in red and gold but not in black and white.

In Test C (black and white trademarks), the Crown in Open has 87% favorable associations and the Crown Inset (which was revised by changing the Crown to gray) has 13% favorable associations. This shows that the revision (gray Crown Inset) does not affect the percentage of favorable associations for the Crown Inset (statistics not shown).

In Test D (red and gold trademarks), the Crown Inset has 20% favorable associations, and the Crown in Open (which was revised by adding red accents to increase visibility and contrast) has 85% favorable associations (statistics not shown).

This shows that the revision of the Crown in Open greatly increases the percentage of favorable associations for the Crown in Open in red and gold. Test A shows that this image is effective in black and white.

In Test E, the revised red and gold Crown in Open (tested by itself) has 90% favorable associations.

CONCLUSION

These tests clearly show that the Crown in Open in red and gold (revised) and in black and white is a very effective marketing tool.

CHAPTER 18

DEVELOPING A PACKAGE WITH THE AID OF RESEARCH

EXECUTIVES of small and middle-size companies often are heard to say that they don't use marketing research because it is too costly. Many don't realize that actually it is much more expensive, in terms of the share of the market, not to use reliable research as a basis for management decision. Those who are aware that a large percentage of sales is the result of impulse buying, and that shoppers buy products because of the quality image of the brand, make use of controlled research as a basis for making marketing decisions.

Coco Wheats is a high quality product of the Little Crow Milling Company. Management wanted an answer to the questions "Does the carton express the high quality of the product? If it does not, what can be done with the carton, so that it would be symbolic of the product's high quality?"

The problem was presented to Color Research Institute with these direct simple questions. There were certain basic steps to be taken in order to get the answers.

Coco Wheats is a typical packaging problem. The report of this study shows how a systematic procedure is used in developing a package that will have maximum marketing effectiveness.

This report shows how ocular measurements—visibility, readability and an eye-movement test—are conducted first of all to determine the display power of the package.

Also worth noting is that the first report includes, in addition to the ocular measurements, ratings of the colors on the package and prescribed colors with preference and retention ratings. The ratings are based on information in our files gathered since 1935.

Only after the design passes the ocular measurements with favorable ratings and the information we have indicates that the colors rate as they should in preference (appeal) and in retention (recall), do we put the package into a field test to determine consumer attitudes.

The report of July 9, 1956, shows how the old Coco Wheats package rates in display effectiveness. (Tables XXXIII, XXXIV and XXXV.) Included are preference, retention and association ratings of the colors. I recommended redesigning the package.

Report of July 23, 1956, shows considerable improvement, but weaknesses are still present. (Table XXXVI.)

Report of November 27, 1956, shows that the package is very effective in display. Visibility and readability are very good. Eye-flow is excellent. (Table XXXVII.)

The report of December 27, 1956, shows that the new package tested by itself has 70% favorable associations, which is high. (Tables XXXVIII and XXXIX.)

Report of January 15, 1957, shows that the new package design, tested against the old package, has 80% favorable associations and the old one 19% favorable associations. (Tables XXXX and XXXXI.)

The tests gave management a basis for making a marketing decision about a package for a high quality product.

Report for LITTLE CROW MILLING COMPANY
Date: July 9, 1956
Subject: OLD COCO WHEATS CARTON

TABLE XXXIII—Ocular Measurements of Old Carton

Test		Ratings
Visibility	—	88
Readability	—COCO WHEATS	76
Eye-movement	—After considerable hesitation, eyes fell on red ribbon, moved down to bowl of Coco Wheats and left package. Attention was not held.	D (Poor)

TABLE XXXIV—Color Ratings

		Ratings
Color preference—Yellow—CCS 2		45
—Red —CCS 12—2+H		88
—Green —CCS 39—b		81
Color retention —Yellow		92
—Red		88
—Green		81
Color association—Yellow		No Rating
—Red	"cooking"	77
	"kitchen"	79
—Green		No Rating

TABLE XXXV—Prescribed Colors

		Ratings
Color preference—Brown	—CCS 10—9	68
—Blue-Green—CCS 35		88
Color retention —Brown		59
—Blue-Green		86

ANALYSIS

The visibility of the Coco Wheats carton is very good.

The brand name readability is fairly good.

However, the front panel does not guide the eyes smoothly and does not hold attention.

Individually, the colors rate high, but they fight for attention and the color of the bowl does nothing for the food in it. (It is optically the wrong color.)

This package is not an effective marketing tool.

I am making specific recommendations for redesigning. It should be understood, however, that a design produced on the basis of my recommendations, like any other design, should be tested to ascertain its effectiveness as a marketing tool.

RECOMMENDATIONS

Specifically, I recommend the following:

1. Get a brand identifying image for the package.
2. Place the bowl of Coco Wheats under COCO WHEATS.
3. Eliminate the red band and put the copy . . . the delicious, etc., under the bowl in brown on yellow.
4. Use a better, richer, higher preference brown.
5. Use a color bowl that is complementary to the Coco Wheats, so that the Coco Wheats is made to look more appetizing.
6. Put the circle with Now! on the left side of the panel.

Send the new design to Color Research Institute for ocular measurements—visibility, readability and eye-movement tests.

Report for LITTLE CROW MILLING COMPANY
Date: July 23, 1956
Subject: NEW COCO WHEATS CARTON DESIGN

TABLE XXXVI—Ocular Measurements of New Design

Test		Ratings
Visibility	—	82
Readability	—COCO WHEATS	84
Eye-movement	—After some hesitation, eyes fell on bowl of Coco Wheats, moved to rectangular panel, to WHEATS to COCO and left package. Attention was held on bowl of Coco Wheats only.	C (Fair)

ANALYSIS

This new design has good visibility and good readability. However, it does not guide the eyes as it should and the upper part of the front panel does not hold attention.

The design should be improved so that eye-flow would be smoother and attention would be held.

Better yet, have the designer make up a box panel on foil according to my recommendations (July 9). Then we will put this foil design through ocular measurements. If it comes out favorably, we will test it in the field with several hundred consumers in a controlled association-type test.

This association test will show consumer attitudes toward the package.

It will reveal specific favorable and/or unfavorable associations with the new foil design and with the present package.

Report for LITTLE CROW MILLING COMPANY
Date: November 27, 1956
Subject: REVISED COCO WHEATS CARTON DESIGN

TABLE XXXVII—Ocular Measurements of Revised Design

Test		Ratings
Visibility	—	86
Readability	—COCO WHEATS	86
Eye-movement	—Eyes fell on COCO WHEATS, moved to bowl, to sticker with *New!*, to *Coco Coated Hot Wheat Cereal* and left package. Attention was held at each point.	A (Excellent)

ANALYSIS

The visibility is very good.

The brand name readability is very good. (It is unusual for the readability and visibility to be the same.)

The design guides the eyes smoothly and holds attention.

Optically, this package is very effective.

RECOMMENDATIONS

I recommend that you get printed proofs or silk screen copies and we put the design into a field test of the association-type with 400 consumers. The association test will reveal consumer attitudes. It will show specific favorable and/or unfavorable associations consumers make with the design. It can be tested by itself and/or against the old package.

Report for LITTLE CROW MILLING COMPANY
Date: December 27, 1956
Association Test: COCO WHEATS PACKAGE DESIGN
Sample: 200 Housewives

**TABLE XXXVIII—Favorable and Unfavorable Associations
(Number and Per Cent)**

	Number	Per Cent
Favorable	959	70%
Unfavorable	412	30%
Total	1371	100%

TABLE XXXIX—Attitudes Ranked

Ranks		
(1)	good	152
(2)	high quality	150
(3)	superior	144
(4)	appetizing	140
(5)	desirable	140
(6)	appealing	138
(7)	for my child	132
(8)	for me	109
(9)	occasional use	101
(10)	everyday use	95
(11)	for my husband	90
(12)	unappetizing	58
(13)	undesirable	55
(14)	unappealing	54
(15)	low quality	50
(16)	inferior	48
(17)	bad	46

ANALYSIS

The Coco Wheats package design received 70% favorable associations.

It is an effective marketing tool.

Report for LITTLE CROW MILLING COMPANY
Date: January 15, 1957
Association Test: NEW DESIGN vs. OLD LABEL (200 Housewives

TABLE XXXX—Favorable and Unfavorable Associations (Number and Per Cent)

	New Design		Old Label	
Favorable	963	80%	233	19%
Unfavorable	235	20%	962	81%
Total	1198	100%	1195	100%

TABLE XXXXI—Attitudes Ranked

Ranks	New Design		Ranks	Old Label	
(1)	desirable	163	(1)	inferior	163
(2)	superior	163	(2)	low quality	162
(3)	high quality	162	(3)	unappetizing	162
(4)	appetizing	162	(4)	undesirable	161
(5)	good	158	(5)	bad	158
(6)	appealing	155	(6)	unappealing	156
(7)	for me	154	(7)	occasional use	95
(8)	everyday use	152	(8)	everyday use	46
(9)	for my child	151	(9)	appealing	44
(10)	for my husband	149	(10)	good	42
(11)	occasional use	99	(11)	for me	42
(12)	unappealing	43	(12)	for my husband	42
(13)	bad	42	(13)	for my child	41
(14)	low quality	38	(14)	high quality	37
(15)	unappetizing	38	(15)	appetizing	37
(16)	undesirable	38	(16)	desirable	37
(17)	inferior	36	(17)	superior	36

ANALYSIS

The New Design received 80% favorable associations and the Present Label received 19%. There were also a large number of associations for the New Design with "everyday use," "for me," "for my husband" and "for my child."

CHAPTER 19

DOES THE AD UPGRADE THE PRODUCT?

PHILIP MORRIS is a company that practices scientific marketing. Its products and its new packages are tested before they are introduced into the market and the ads are tested as soon as they are available for testing.

George Weissman, Merchandising Vice President, chooses the research to fit the problem. Color Research Institute is used for testing packages and ads.

Jet Lincoln is in charge of all research activities. He is a marketing research analyst in his own right. I analyze the research results in broad terms; he dips deep into the special statistical breakdowns, which he orders, and which have significant meaning to him in relation to market planning. I had many occasions to see how meaningful statistics are to him.

We test ads in a number of ways.

1. The ad is put through an eye-movement test.

2. The ad is submitted to a controlled association test that reveals percentage of favorable and of unfavorable attitudes.

3. The package is tested in the presence of the ad. The results of this test are compared with those of the package test, to see whether the ad upgrades or downgrades the package.

4. The package is tested in the presence of the ad, against a competitive package. The results of this test are compared with the results of the package test, against a competitive package in which the ad is not involved, to see whether the ad upgrades or downgrades the package.

5. The product is tested in the presence of the ad, against a competitive product. The results of this test are compared with the results of a product test, against a competitive product in which the ad is not included, to see whether the ad upgrades or downgrades the product.

In a product ad test, the respondents are asked to taste or to use the product being tested and the competitive product.

No special skills are needed for conducting Test No. 1. All one needs is the instrument.

Conducting Tests No. 2, No. 3, No. 4 and No. 5 requires great know-how and many controls. These are not the kinds of tests that can be conducted by amateur researchers. Strictly controlled conditions must prevail in conducting such tests. Controls must be used in the design of the test, in the consumer sampling, and in administering it. The indirect approach is vital. Traditional, direct testing methods are not applicable here.

Three Philip Morris cigarette tests are shown in part on the following pages.

A. Percentage of favorable attitudes toward the Philip Morris package and toward a competitive package. (Tables XXXXII and XXXXIII.)

B. Attitudes toward the Philip Morris ad, "Pardon Us While We Change Our Dress," that introduced the new Philip Morris package. (Tables XXXXIV and XXXXV.)

C. Percentage of favorable attitudes toward the Philip Morris package and toward a competitive package, while the respondents were exposed to the Philip Morris ad, "Pardon Us While We Change Our Dress." (Tables XXXXVI and XXXXVII.)

Only a small part of the study is reproduced here. Test A showed that the new Philip Morris cigarette package was slightly better than the competitive brand, with 3% advantage in favorable associations. Philip Morris was just a little better in association with "mild" and "cool." It was significantly better in association with "clean."

In Test B, the ad "Pardon Us While We Change Our Dress" received 64% favorable associations.

In Test C, the Philip Morris cigarettes in the presence of the ad "Pardon Us While We Change Our Dress," rated 61% in favorable associations and the competitive brand only 39%. Without the ad Philip Morris had an advantage of 3% favorable associations; with the ad, the advantage increased to 22% favorable associations. Philip Morris rated much higher in this test than did the competitive brand in association with "mild," "cool" and "high quality tobacco."

The result of an effective ad is clearly illustrated here.

Report for PHILIP MORRIS, INC.

Date: September 15, 1955

Association Test: NEW PHILIP MORRIS PACKAGE vs.
                  COMPETITIVE BRAND (450 Cigarette Smokers)

TABLE XXXXII—Test A: Favorable and Unfavorable Associations (Number and Per Cent)

	Attitudes Toward Cigarettes			
	Philip Morris		Competitive Brand	
Favorable	1621	52%	1527	49%
Unfavorable	1499	48%	1601	51%
Total	3120	100%	3128	100%

TABLE XXXXIII—Test A: Number of Associations with Attitude Words

	Attitudes Toward Cigarettes	
Favorable	Philip Morris	Competitive Brand
mild	230	219
cool	231	219
not irritating	228	222
high quality tobacco	225	225
good flavor	225	225
clean	252	197
exciting	230	220
Total	1621	1527
Unfavorable		
strong	219	229
hot	217	230
irritating	221	228
low quality tobacco	222	221
poor flavor	223	220
not clean	190	246
dull	207	227
Total	1499	1601
Grand Total	3120	3128

Report for PHILIP MORRIS, INC.

Date: September 15, 1955

Association Test: NEW PHILIP MORRIS PACKAGE vs. COMPETITIVE BRAND
(with Philip Morris Ad—"Pardon Us While We Change Our Dress")

Sample: 453 Cigarette Smokers

TABLE XXXXIV—Test B: Favorable and Unfavorable Associations (Number and Per Cent)

	Attitudes Toward Ad					
	Men (226)		Women (227)		Total (453)	
Favorable	805	72%	628	55%	1433	64%
Unfavorable	318	28%	505	45%	823	36%
Total	1123	100%	1133	100%	2256	100%

TABLE XXXXV—Test B: Number of Associations with Attitude Words

	Men (226)	Women (227)	Total (453)
Favorable			
good	182	166	348
appealing	184	154	338
important	107	51	158
interesting	188	148	336
for me	144	109	253
Total	805	628	1433
Unfavorable			
bad	40	61	101
unappealing	41	72	113
unimportant	117	175	292
uninteresting	38	79	117
not for me	82	118	200
Total	318	505	823
Grand Total	1123	1133	2256

TABLE XXXXVI—Test C: Favorable and Unfavorable Associations (Number and Per Cent)

Attitudes Toward Cigarettes (in presence of Ad)				
	Philip Morris		Competitive Brand	
Favorable	1938	61%	1230	39%
Unfavorable	1221	39%	1925	61%
Total	3159	100%	3155	100%

TABLE XXXXVII—Test C: Number of Associations with Attitude Words

Attitudes Toward Cigarettes (in presence of Ad)	Philip Morris	Competitive Brand
Favorable		
mild	263	189
cool	269	183
not irritating	281	171
high quality tobacco	281	171
good flavor	287	166
clean	287	169
exciting	270	181
Total	1938	1230
Unfavorable		
strong	189	263
hot	173	278
irritating	172	277
low quality tobacco	176	276
poor flavor	167	282
not clean	167	276
dull	177	273
Total	1221	1925
Grand Total	3159	3155

CHAPTER 20

GIVING CONSUMERS WHAT THEY WANT

ALMOST all managers are aware of the value of their employees' time. Many have developed or purchased devices for saving time and for increasing the efficiency of employees. However, many top executives think it perfectly normal to spend a day around a conference table, in a committee meeting, discussing what housewives will or will not buy.

The fact that not a single one of them could possibly react to any object as a typical housewife would, does not seem to occur to them. What is more, they spend costly time trying to "guess" the answer to a problem for which they can get the right answer through research, for a few hundred dollars.

Once, I calculated the cost of choosing a design by a committee of executives. I was provided with the information on salaries of all the members of the committee and I was given a time sheet on the hours that were spent in conferences on the specific problem. The cost was $58,000.00.

The following year the problem was submitted to Color Research Institute for research. The cost of the research was $1750.00 and management spent $1100.00 in time, in decision making. Total cost of arriving at a marketing decision was, therefore, $2850.00. It meant a saving of over $55,000.00. What is more, the decision that was made on the basis of research led to a much more successful marketing program.

One company that does not waste the time of executives in trying to "guess" what consumers want is Consoweld Corporation. The executives of this company use controlled research to find out whether consumers react favorably or unfavorably to a design.

Consoweld is a plastic laminate used for table tops, kitchen counters, kitchen wainscoting, lunch counters, dinette table tops, bathroom and recreation room walls, etc. Producing a pattern that has little consumer acceptance means an inventory problem and a great loss.

In 1954, the Consoweld Corporation began a study of its entire line. Color Research Institute was employed to provide information on color and design for Consoweld plastic laminates.

Because plastic laminates are used along with other furnishings in a kitchen, dinette, bathroom, recreation room, etc., a color system was adopted for the Consoweld line. Color charts were produced to be used as an aid in planning interiors. There are 12 color charts and there are Consoweld patterns that match colors on each chart. The color charts are the same as those in the book *How to Color-Tune Your Home.*

Most of the colors for Consoweld were chosen on the basis of available information in our files. Some of the colors were tested in the field with potential users of the product. All the designs were put into field tests with potential users of the product.

On the basis of the information we had on the colors and on the basis of the test results, inventory was cut in half. Management concentrated on selling high preference patterns and colors. Sales doubled in about a year. A new plant was built and a program of testing each new design became a regular procedure.

A few of the reports on tests of designs are reproduced here. They show clearly that some patterns have low preference and some high appeal. For example, in the report of November 28, 1955, Pattern 1 is definitely one that is not to be put into production. Pattern 5 is another very poor pattern, and Pattern 8 is not good enough. Pattern 10, with only 17% favorable associations, is clearly not a pattern that has appeal. (Table XXXXIX.)

The report of November 22, 1957, is a very interesting one because Mosaic, a new pattern, was tested against two top selling patterns, Marble and Pearl. Needless to say, after the test results were seen, the Mosaic was immediately added to the line. (Tables L, LI, LII, and LIII.)

The Marble and Mosaic came out much better in the pink color, than they did in green. The Pearl came out much better in green than it did in pink.

The report of July 17, 1958, is also a very interesting one. It shows that Pink Plaza has much greater acceptance than Pink Holiday. And Plaza also rates higher than Holiday in Lime color. Yet Holiday was a successful pattern. (Tables LIV, LV, LVI, and LVII.)

Consoweld is a Corporation practicing scientific marketing. The emphasis is not on the company selling, but on the consumer buying. The executives use research to find out what the consumer wants, and what he does not want. They manufacture only the patterns and colors that the consumer wants.

This is a consumer oriented company. Top management, sales management, advertising and production, and the creative department personnel are all consumer oriented. The executives have decision-making conferences. The decisions are based on objective information of consumer interests and wants.

Report for CONSOWELD CORPORATION
Date: July 26, 1954
Association Test: FOUR LAMINATED PLASTIC PATTERNS (200 Women)

TABLE XXXXVIII—Number of Associations with Attitude Words

	Bandbox 1	Mardi Gras 2	Holiday 3	Skylark 4
appealing	47	55	91	27
unappealing	91	35	31	60
cheap	81	15	31	41
expensive	43	48	61	32
commonplace	87	32	31	29
unusual	43	55	49	76
modern	72	44	63	81
informal	75	39	53	25
sophisticated	33	39	55	52
gay	16	55	120	23
beautiful	17	27	56	21
smart	53	40	75	37
fresh	33	44	75	24
gaudy	47	25	37	67
kitchen counters	73	44	49	31
bathroom counter	55	43	56	29
dinette table	40	52	64	29
cocktail table	28	49	49	61
playroom walls	71	31	53	36
rumpus room walls	61	33	48	48
Total	1066	805	1147	829

ANALYSIS

The Association Test reveals very significant consumer reactions.

In impact which is revealed by the total number of tallies, the Holiday Pattern (3) is the strongest and Bandbox (1) is a close second. Mardi Gras (2) and Skylark (4) are weak, in that many consumers did not react to them either favorably or unfavorably.

The association with appealing is very important. Holiday (3) has 91 tallies. Skylark has only 27 tallies. Bandbox and Mardi Gras have 47 and 55.

Unappealing has fewest tallies in association with Holiday (3).

It is significant that Bandbox (1) goes up in association with kitchen counters and playroom walls. But Holiday (3) maintains itself for every other purpose.

In short, the test shows that Holiday (3) has the greatest impact (1147 tallies) and the greatest number of favorable associations.

Skylark (4) although it rates high with modern and unusual, is the weakest of the four in appeal.

The consumers' associations of the patterns with the names are also enlightening. They confirm the appropriateness of the names derived from the original design name tests. In other words, the names Bandbox for Pattern 1, Mardi Gras for Pattern 2, and Holiday for Pattern 3 are appropriate. (Statistics not shown.)

Report for CONSOWELD CORPORATION
Date: November 28, 1955
Association Tests: TWELVE DINETTE PATTERNS

**TABLE XXXXIX—Favorable and Unfavorable Associations
(Number and Per Cent)**

Test 1—Color Group I—Four Patterns			Sample: 200 Consumers
	Pattern 1	Pattern 2	Pattern 3	Pattern 4
Favorable	224	520	584	615
Unfavorable	770	393	325	373
Total	994	913	909	988
Favorable	23%	57%	64%	62%
Unfavorable	77%	43%	36%	38%
Total	100%	100%	100%	100%

Test 2—Color Group II—Four Patterns			Sample: 200 Consumers
	Pattern 5	Pattern 6	Pattern 7	Pattern 8
Favorable	284	619	716	366
Unfavorable	728	440	272	557
Total	1012	1059	988	923
Favorable	28%	58%	72%	40%
Unfavorable	72%	42%	28%	60%
Total	100%	100%	100%	100%

Test 3—Color Group III—Four Patterns			Sample: 200 Consumers
	Pattern 9	Pattern 10	Pattern 11	Pattern 12
Favorable	570	141	676	416
Unfavorable	299	678	201	519
Total	869	819	877	935
Favorable	66%	17%	77%	44%
Unfavorable	34%	83%	23%	56%
Total	100%	100%	100%	100%

ANALYSIS

Test 1—Color Group I—Four Patterns

This test shows that Patterns 3 and 4 are very good; Pattern 2 is good and Pattern 1 is poor.

Test 2—Color Group II—Four Patterns

This test shows that Pattern 7 is excellent; Pattern 6 is good; Patterns 5 and 8 are poor.

Test 3—Color Group III—Four Patterns

This test shows that Pattern 11 is excellent; Pattern 9 is very good. Patterns 10 and 12 are poor.

Report for CONSOWELD CORPORATION
Date: November 22, 1957
Association Tests: MARBLE vs. MOSAIC vs. PEARL

TABLE L—Favorable and Unfavorable Associations

Test A—Pink					Sample: 403 Consumers	
	Marble		Mosaic		Pearl	
Favorable	533	39%	790	54%	725	59%
Unfavorable	823	61%	672	46%	505	41%
Total	1356	100%	1462	100%	1230	100%

Test B—Green					Sample: 400 Consumers	
	Marble		Mosaic		Pearl	
Favorable	259	21%	660	49%	1079	78%
Unfavorable	969	79%	700	51%	309	22%
Total	1228	100%	1360	100%	1388	100%

Test C—Tan					Sample: 403 Consumers	
	Marble		Mosaic		Pearl	
Favorable	388	30%	813	56%	774	65%
Unfavorable	916	70%	642	44%	412	35%
Total	1304	100%	1455	100%	1186	100%

TABLE LI—Number of Associations with Attitude Words

	Test A—Pink		
	Marble	Mosaic	Pearl
Favorable			
good	108	155	153
high quality	111	155	148
attractive	98	176	137
expensive	102	155	144
for me *	114	149	143
Total	533	790	725
Unfavorable			
bad	164	141	95
low quality	166	125	105
unattractive	159	148	101
cheap	168	129	98
not for me	166	129	106
Total	823	672	505

* Preference

	Marble	Mosaic	Pearl
Unclassified			
bathroom walls	195	91	96
kitchen wainscotting	145	140	114
vanity tops	117	117	150
kitchen counters	93	141	167
dinette table tops	109	95	189
lunch counter	106	151	145

284

TABLE LII—Number of Associations with Attitude Words

	Test B—Green		
	Marble	Mosaic	Pearl
Favorable			
good	50	146	212
high quality	58	130	222
attractive	52	137	215
expensive	53	127	215
for me *	46	120	215
Total	259	660	1079
Unfavorable			
bad	193	136	61
low quality	198	137	55
unattractive	187	146	59
cheap	197	142	63
not for me	194	139	71
Total	969	700	309

* Preference

	Marble	Mosaic	Pearl
Unclassified			
bathroom walls	125	78	196
kitchen wainscotting	70	113	213
vanity tops	85	110	198
kitchen counters	67	122	215
dinette table tops	68	103	228
lunch counter	63	132	207

LOUIS CHESKIN

TABLE LIII—Number of Associations with Attitude Words

| | Test C—Tan | | |
	Marble	Mosaic	Pearl
Favorable			
good	72	175	147
high quality	76	147	174
attractive	82	177	140
expensive	73	164	158
for me *	85	150	155
Total	388	813	774
Unfavorable			
bad	184	141	75
low quality	186	116	86
unattractive	186	130	80
cheap	181	122	88
not for me	179	133	83
Total	916	642	412

* Preference

	Marble	Mosaic	Pearl
Unclassified			
bathroom walls	127	180	92
kitchen wainscotting	87	138	170
vanity tops	142	89	164
kitchen counters	61	127	207
dinette table tops	73	120	200
lunch counter	72	150	174

220

ANALYSIS

In Test A (Pink) Marble has 39% favorable associations, Mosaic 54% and Pearl 59%. In Test B (Green) Marble has 21%, Mosaic 49% and Pearl 78%. In Test C (Tan) Marble has 30%, Mosaic 56% and Pearl 65%.

With specific applications the Marble pattern has the largest number of associations in Pink and Green with bathroom walls and in Tan with vanity tops.

The Pearl pattern has the largest number of associations in Pink and Green with dinette table tops and in Tan with kitchen counters.

The Mosaic pattern has the largest number of associations in Pink and Green with lunch counter, and in Tan with bathroom walls.

These tests show that the Mosaic is an effective pattern, indeed. It is almost as effective as the Pearl and more effective than the Marble, both well-established patterns.

Report for CONSOWELD CORPORATION
Date: July 17, 1958
Association Tests: PLAZA vs. HOLIDAY

Test 1: Pink—305 Consumers Test 2: Lime—301 Consumers

TABLE LIV—Test 1: Favorable and Unfavorable Associations (Number and Per Cent)

	Pink Plaza	Pink Holiday
Favorable	1430	690
Unfavorable	695	1419
Total	2125	2109
Favorable	67%	33%
Unfavorable	33%	67%
Total	100%	100%

TABLE LV—Test 1: Attitudes Ranked

Ranks	Pink Plaza		Ranks	Pink Holiday	
(1)	appealing	210	(1)	not for me	208
(2)	for me	207	(2)	cheap	204
(3)	expensive	206	(3)	unappealing	204
(4)	good	205	(4)	low quality	204
(5)	attractive	205	(5)	bad	203
(6)	high quality	204	(6)	unattractive	203
(7)	high class	193	(7)	low class	193
(8)	kitchen wainscotting	178	(8)	lunch counter	163
(9)	bathroom walls	172	(9)	dinette table tops	151
(10)	kitchen counters	169	(10)	vanity tops	148
(11)	vanity tops	156	(11)	kitchen counters	135
(12)	dinette table tops	154	(12)	bathroom walls	133
(13)	lunch counter	142	(13)	kitchen wainscotting	129
(14)	low class	112	(14)	high class	111
(15)	unattractive	100	(15)	good	100
(16)	bad	99	(16)	high quality	99
(17)	low quality	97	(17)	attractive	98
(18)	unappealing	96	(18)	for me	96
(19)	cheap	96	(19)	expensive	93
(20)	not for me	95	(20)	appealing	93

Table LVI—Test 2: Favorable and Unfavorable Associations
(Number and Per Cent)

	Lime Plaza	Lime Holiday
Favorable	1425	675
Unfavorable	605	1195
Total	2030	1870
Favorable	70%	36%
Unfavorable	30%	64%
Total	100%	100%

TABLE LVII—Test 2: Attitudes Ranked

Ranks	Lime Plaza		Ranks	Lime Holiday	
(1)	good	209	(1)	unappealing	201
(2)	appealing	206	(2)	unattractive	199
(3)	attractive	205	(3)	not for me	195
(4)	high class	205	(4)	cheap	152
(5)	high quality	204	(5)	low quality	151
(6)	for me	204	(6)	bad	149
(7)	expensive	192	(7)	low class	148
(8)	dinette table tops	188	(8)	lunch counter	119
(9)	kitchen wainscotting	182	(9)	kitchen counters	118
(10)	kitchen counters	178	(10)	vanity tops	118
(11)	bathroom walls	177	(11)	bathroom walls	116
(12)	lunch counter	174	(12)	kitchen wainscotting	112
(13)	vanity tops	173	(13)	dinette table tops	105
(14)	unappealing	95	(14)	high quality	103
(15)	unattractive	95	(15)	expensive	102
(16)	low quality	89	(16)	attractive	97
(17)	not for me	89	(17)	appealing	96
(18)	cheap	86	(18)	high class	95
(19)	low class	76	(19)	good	93
(20)	bad	75	(20)	for me	89

ANALYSIS

Test 1

The Pink Plaza has 67% favorable associations and the Pink Holiday has 33%.

Test 2

The Lime Plaza has 70% favorable associations and the Lime Holiday, 36%.

CHAPTER 21

THE IMAGE OF A WOMEN'S APPAREL STORE

THE MANAGERS of a community women's apparel store came to Color Research Institute with the following questions. "How do people in our neighborhood classify us? What do they think of us? In our store operation where are we weak and where are we strong?" Reproduced here is part of the report on the study of the store. Two other stores were used as controls, one very successful "prestige shop" and a well-known department store.

The results of this study served as a basis for management decision in setting future policies in the operation of the store.

Report for STORE A
Date: April 15, 1958
Association Test: CONSUMER ATTITUDES TOWARD STORE A
Sample: 50 Customers of Store A and 150 Women from Area

TABLE LVIII—Favorable and Unfavorable Associations
(Number and Per Cent)

Sample: 50 Customers of Store A						
	Store A		Control Store 1		Control Store 2	
Favorable	358	94%	212	70%	180	72%
Unfavorable	22	6%	92	30%	69	28%
Total	380	100%	304	100%	249	100%

TABLE LIX—Per Cent of Associations with Attitude Words

Sample: 50 Customers of Store A

	Store A	Control Store 1	Control Store 2
friendly	98%	68%	46%
unfriendly	0%	12%	12%
good selection	92%	52%	56%
poor selection	4%	22%	0%
not too expensive	64%	80%	10%
too expensive	14%	0%	58%
high class	66%	4%	60%
low class	4%	32%	0%
more for your money	24%	58%	10%
less for your money	16%	14%	18%
pleasant surroundings	92%	60%	56%
unpleasant surroundings	0%	10%	2%
helpful salespeople	90%	54%	30%
annoying salespeople	4%	14%	6%
fashionable	94%	24%	64%
not fashionable	2%	28%	0%
young women	28%	6%	8%
mature women	12%	14%	8%
all women	60%	74%	42%
street dresses	74%	54%	26%
dressy dresses	82%	12%	50%
suits	76%	20%	38%
blouses	64%	34%	28%
sweaters	76%	38%	28%
skirts	78%	30%	28%
coats	84%	20%	30%
for me	96%	24%	28%
not for me	0%	52%	42%

LOUIS CHESKIN

TABLE LX—Favorable and Unfavorable Associations

Sample: 150 Women from Store A Trading Area

	Store A		Control Store 1		Control Store 2	
Favorable	923	75%	934	73%	833	69%
Unfavorable	310	25%	342	27%	368	31%
Total	1233	100%	1276	100%	1201	100%

TABLE LXI—Per Cent of Associations with Attitude Words

	Store A	Store 1	Store 2
friendly	80%	95%	59%
unfriendly	12%	5%	27%
good selection	71%	72%	74%
poor selection	19%	22%	7%
not too expensive	49%	91%	26%
too expensive	49%	8%	73%
high class	73%	23%	80%
low class	19%	69%	11%
more for your money	41%	69%	34%
less for your money	43%	26%	51%
pleasant surroundings	78%	78%	75%
unpleasant surroundings	8%	9%	9%
helpful salespeople	71%	81%	61%
annoying salespeople	15%	9%	20%
fashionable	83%	50%	91%
not fashionable	13%	45%	4%
young women	61%	42%	59%
mature women	41%	58%	53%
all women	27%	61%	30%
street dresses	63%	73%	51%
dressy dresses	68%	31%	73%
suits	69%	49%	65%
blouses	51%	60%	37%
sweaters	60%	65%	39%
skirts	52%	59%	30%
coats	55%	30%	67%
for me	69%	64%	55%
not for me	29%	35%	44%

ANALYSIS

Store A has 94% total favorable association with the 50 women who are Store A customers. It has 75% total favorable association with the 150 women who live in the Store A trading area.

Control Store 1 has 70% total favorable association with the Store A customers and 73% total favorable association with the women from the trading area.

Control Store 2 has 72% total favorable association with the Store A customers and 69% favorable association with the women from the trading area.

The 50 Store A customers rate Store A highest in association with "friendly" (98%), "for me" (96%), "fashionable" (94%), "good selection" (92%), "pleasant surroundings" (92%), and "helpful salespeople" (90%).

The 150 women from the trading area rate Store A highest in association with "fashionable" (83%), "friendly" (80%), "pleasant surroundings" (78%), "high class" (73%), "helpful salespeople" (71%) and "good selection" (71%).

In all favorable attitudes except "high class" and "more for your money" the Store A customers rate Store A higher than did the women from the Store A trading area.

Many of the Store A customers did not respond to the attitudes "more for your money" or "less for your money," while most of the 150 women from the trading area responded.

The low percentage of association (27%) with "for all women" indicates that most of the women from the trading area feel that Store A appeals to a certain age group of women, but not to all women. Of the Store A customers, 60% feel that the store appeals to all women.

The Store A customers rate Store A higher than both Control Store 1 and Control Store 2 in all favorable attitudes except "not too expensive" and "more for your money."

LOUIS CHESKIN

With "not too expensive" and "more for your money," Control Store 1 is rated highest.

The women from the trading area rate Control Store 1 higher than Store A or Control Store 2 with "friendly," "not too expensive," "more for your money," and "helpful salespeople."

The women from the trading area rate Control Store 2 higher than Store A or Control Store 1 with "high class" and "fashionable." However, the women from the trading area rate Store A higher than Control Store 1 or Control Store 2 with "for me."

This indicates that although the women from the trading area do not rate Store A as high in each attitude as do the Store A customers, they still find in Store A an image that they want to identify themselves with.

The test shows that Store A rates very high in quality and service connotations (fashionable, helpful salespeople, etc.) with both the Store A customers and the women from the trading area and in general presents a favorable image to both groups.

If there is any weakness in the Store A marketing program, it is not in the consumer image of the store. This test shows clearly that the store image has favorable connotations.

CHAPTER 22

SCIENTIFIC MARKETING OF BREAD AND OIL

MARKETING information is of a highly confidential nature. The meaningful marketing findings from research conducted for a client belong to the client. The final results of a study cannot be released to the public as long as those results are of value to the client.

Parts of the original reports to our clients had to be eliminated for the following reasons:

In some cases, the report revealed marketing information which could not be disclosed because it may still be of value to the client.

The primary purpose of this book is not to show test results, but to show how controlled research is used by "scientific-minded" management as a basis for making marketing decisions.

The objective is also to show examples of reports of studies that are conducted under controlled conditions.

The partial reports show ocular measurement ratings, the use of the semantic differential and the statistical structure of controlled association tests.

Many marketing successes that have been predicted by Color Research Institute tests are covered in *How to Predict What People Will Buy*. There is, therefore, no reason for discussing them in this book.

The fact that The Procter & Gamble Company is a pioneer in scientific marketing is no secret to anyone. The first studies for The Procter & Gamble Company were made by Color Research Institute in 1947. Labels for Crisco were the first assignment. However, there are companies, who do not have as great a variety of consumer products as The Procter & Gamble Company, who pioneered scientific marketing in their fields.

There was a great temptation to show reports of studies of brassieres and shoes, eggs and turkeys, sports clothes and fishing rods, salad dressings and desserts, seed packages and lawn mowers, cooking fuel and refrigerators, small shops and department stores, and also non-motivating ads as well as motivating ads.

I wanted to show more studies that were conducted for advertising agencies. There are a number of very interesting tests that were done for the Gardner Advertising Company of St. Louis. I considered including some wonderful studies made for Morey, Humm & Warwick, New York. We have recently completed studies for the Dubin Advertising Agency, Pittsburgh, of Kaycrest brand-identifying images and packages. (Kaycrest of The Papercraft Corporation now has a symbol in keeping with the character and quality of Kaycrest products, gift wrapping papers.) The Mautner Advertising Agency of Milwaukee has also brought us some interesting projects. We have conducted studies for other agencies. However, a book by its nature is limited in scope and in size and I must therefore conclude with only two more examples of scientific marketing—bread and oil.

QBA

The management of Quality Bakers of America Cooperative, Inc. became interested in motivation research about ten years before the publication of this book. Robert Schaus, Advertising Manager of QBA, merchandisers of Sunbeam bread and other bakery products, presented a marketing problem to us in 1949.

At the same time, he presented the problem to another motivation research organization. This I learned after our study was completed. The results of the findings of the two studies are marketing history. The directors of QBA, J. P. Duchaine, President, George N. Graf, General Manager and Robert Schaus, Director of Advertising had a scientific attitude toward marketing as far back as 1949. They knew then, that for successful marketing, it was vital to find out what motivates consumers.

In 1949, they knew that you could not interview housewives and ask them to tell how they react to a package.

These studies served as a basis for making marketing decisions by the scientifically-minded management of QBA.

The ocular measurements report (1950) that follows is of the old bread wrapper. On the basis of the ocular measurements and color and image ratings, QBA had new Sunbeam bread wrappers designed. Six of the new designs came out excellent in the visibility, readability and eye-movement measurements. The association test reproduced here (1951) shows consumer attitudes toward the six designs without either product or brand identity. The last report (1958), shown in part, is of an association test in which a QBA ad received 88% favorable associations.

Report for QUALITY BAKERS OF AMERICA
Date: November 15, 1950
Subject: SUNBEAM BREAD WRAPPER (small loaf)

TABLE LXII—Ocular Measurements

Test		Ratings
Visibility	—	74
Readability	—	69
Eye-movement	—Eyes fell on Miss Sunbeam figure where attention was held, then moved to SUNBEAM and to the end of the package where gaze dropped off.	A (Excellent)

TABLE LXIII—Image and Color Ratings

		Ratings
Image preference	—Miss Sunbeam	99
Image retention	—Miss Sunbeam	99
Color preference	—Blue (CCS 32) (halftone)	93
	—Blue (CCS 28 + Hue) (solid)	85
	—Red (CCS 11 + Hue)	89
	—Yellow (CCS 1+ 2)	78
Color retention	—Blue (halftone)	83
	—Blue (solid)	80
	—Red	99
	—Yellow	94
Image symbolism	—Miss Sunbeam (in association with happy child)	100
Color symbolism	—	None

Report for QUALITY BAKERS OF AMERICA
Date: September 10, 1951
Association Test: SIX BREAD WRAPPER DESIGNS (335 Housewives)

TABLE LXIV—Per Cent of Associations with Attitude Words

	No. 1	No. 2	No. 3	No. 4	No. 5	No. 6
delicate	2%	0%	30%	65%	0%	2%
strong	25%	20%	3%	3%	27%	22%
soft	5%	2%	28%	45%	2%	17%
harsh	21%	21%	3%	3%	37%	15%
pretty	2%	2%	33%	60%	1%	2%
ugly	28%	23%	2%	1%	24%	22%
food	3%	4%	45%	35%	4%	9%
sport	21%	9%	0%	4%	34%	32%
masculine	7%	20%	0%	0%	36%	37%
feminine	2%	2%	38%	55%	1%	2%
library	1%	6%	6%	8%	65%	15%
dining room	24%	15%	32%	14%	9%	6%
breakfast	10%	20%	35%	18%	9%	8%
tavern	25%	27%	4%	3%	27%	14%
lunch	4%	16%	34%	26%	5%	14%
game	20%	14%	1%	1%	31%	32%
bread	3%	35%	8%	8%	25%	22%
ball	21%	35%	12%	10%	13%	10%
good	6%	13%	15%	27%	6%	33%
bad	41%	17%	2%	1%	31%	10%

Report for QUALITY BAKERS OF AMERICA
Date: May 19, 1958
Association Test: SUNBEAM BREAD AD (303 Housewives)

TABLE LXV—Favorable and Unfavorable Associations

	Number	Per Cent
Favorable	3190	88%
Unfavorable	419	12%
Total	3609	100%

Table LXVI—Number of Associations with Attitude Words

	Number
Favorable	
good	278
nutritious	267
healthful	286
desirable	265
high quality	252
appealing	265
high in vitamins	270
good body-builder	278
more wholesome	275
superior	255
full of energy	281
for me	218
Total	3190
Unfavorable	
bad	23
not nutritious	32
not healthful	15
undesirable	36
low quality	48
unappealing	37
low in vitamins	30
poor body-builder	23
less wholesome	26
inferior	45
not full of energy	20
not for me	84
Total	419
Grand Total	3609

Pioneer in Scientific Marketing

ONE OF THE outstanding figures among the pioneers of scientific marketing is Wesley I. Nunn, Advertising Manager of Standard Oil Company of Indiana.

There are still many marketing men who do not know what scientific marketing is, but even in progressive marketing circles, it is commonly believed that scientific marketing applies only to the super market.

It is widely known that since 1945, Color Research Institute has been playing a vital role in the field of developing marketing tools, particularly packages and brand-identifying images for food products, soaps and toiletries. Few are aware that scientific marketing was also pioneered in fields that are not connected with the super market.

The symbol (oval with torch) of the Standard Oil Company of Indiana was developed by creative people with the aid of objective research, under the direction of Wesley Nunn, almost fifteen years ago when scientific marketing was at the pioneering stage.

The following is part of the report of a study made in August of 1945 on the Standard Oil brand-identifying image. The study showed that the Standard "sign" was a most effective symbol.

Studies, that have been completed in 1959, show that the Standard sign is still one of the most effective brand-identifying images on the American scene.

The part of the 1945 study of the brand symbol of the Standard Oil Company of Indiana is reproduced here in its original form.

Report for STANDARD OIL COMPANY of INDIANA
Date: August 13, 1945
Subject: STANDARD OIL SIGNS

PROBLEM

To determine which of four sign designs is the most effective and how the most effective sign can be improved in design and color to fulfill the purpose most effectively.

The design should have:

1. Greatest visibility under all weather conditions.
2. Lettering readable at greatest possible distance.
3. Maximum effectiveness as an emblem on packaging, advertising, etc.
4. Most appropriate symbol for expressing the character of the company.

TESTS

Designs Nos. 290, 295, 296 and 299 were put to the following eighteen tests on visibility and readability.

Tests 1 to 5: Visibility under normal conditions—bright day
(made at 9 AM, 12:30 PM, 2 PM, 5 PM and 8 PM). The same results were found in all five tests:

> Design No. 290 had the greatest visibility.
>
> Design No. 296 had second greatest visibility.
>
> Design No. 295 had third greatest visibility.
>
> Design No. 299 had the least visibility.

Test 6: Visibility under smoky conditions.

> Design No. 296 had greatest visibility.
>
> Design No. 290 had second greatest visibility.
>
> Design No. 295 had third greatest visibility.
>
> Design No. 299 had the least visibility.

Test 7: Visibility indoors under artificial lighting conditions (10 foot-candles).

> Design No. 296 had greatest visibility.
>
> Design No. 290 had second greatest visibility.
>
> Design No. 295 had third greatest visibility.
>
> Design No. 299 had the least visibility.

Test 8 to 13: Readability tests of word STANDARD under normal conditions—bright day (made at 9 AM, 12:30 PM, 2 PM, 5 PM and 8 PM. The same time as the visibility tests). The same results were found in all five tests.

> Design No. 290 was readable at greatest distance.
>
> Design No. 299 was readable at second greatest distance.
>
> Design No. 295 was readable at third greatest distance.
>
> Design No. 296 was readable at the shortest distance.

Test 14: Readability tests under smoky conditions showed the same results as above.

Test 13: Readability of word STANDARD under artificial lighting conditions (10 foot-candles).

> Design No. 290 was readable at 80 feet.
>
> Design No. 299 was readable at 75 feet.
>
> Design No. 295 was readable at 70 feet.
>
> Design No. 296 was readable at 60 feet.

Test 16: Readability meter test of word STANDARD (Readability of sign at 20 feet is equal to readability of type at 14 inches).

> Design Nos. 299 and 290 have the readability of 12 point type (Bodoni Book).
>
> Design No. 295 has the readability of 11 point type.
>
> Design No. 296 has the readability of 9 point type.

Test 17: Visibility of Colors—blue and red under normal lighting conditions.

Red on Design No. 296 had best visibility.

Red on Design No. 290 had the second best visibility.

Red on Design No. 295 had the third best visibility.

Red on Design No. 299 had the least visibility.

The blue on each of the signs produced the same results.

Test 18: Visibility of Colors—blue and red under smoky conditions.

The results were the same as under normal light.

ANALYSIS OF SYMBOLIC VALUE OF DESIGN, COLOR, LETTERING OF ALL FOUR SIGNS

Design No. 296 has two symbolic values, the color and the torch, whereas the other three designs each have only the color symbolizing the company.

Lower case lettering has greater readability than capitals, but lower case letters do not have the strength of character of capitals. Capital letters express strength, unity, quality, and dignity.

The symbolic power of capital letters is also a factor to be considered. Capital letters are formal and symmetrical. Design No. 296 is symmetrical and capital letters are, therefore, appropriate for it.

SOLVING THE PROBLEM

The series of tests have shown Design No. 296 to be superior in every way except in readability of the word STANDARD. The problem is to improve the readability of the word STANDARD on Design No. 296.

Lower case letters would undoubtedly improve the readability but would sacrifice design quality. It was, therefore, decided to find a way of improving the readability of the capital letters.

A new design (similar to No. 296) was made (No. 296L), and three strips with the word STANDARD were made. Strip one, with lettering about

14 of an inch higher than in Design No. 296, same width. Strip two, with lettering 14 of an inch higher than in Design No. 296, but much narrower, allowing more open space between the letters. Strip three with lettering same height as on Design No. 296 but much narrower letters, allowing more open space between letters.

Tests 20 to 22: Readability tests of the three new strips of lettering of STANDARD (made indoors—lighting 20 foot-candles, outdoors—9 AM, and outdoors—twilight).

Strip three had the best readability in all three tests.

Test 23: Readability tests of Designs No. 290 (best in readability), *No. 296* (best design), *and No. 296L* (new sign with strip three lettering). Made outdoors at 5:30 PM on sidewalk near building on the east side.

Design No. 290 was readable at 76 feet.

Design No. 296L was readable at 67 feet.

Design No. 296 was readable at 56 feet.

Test 24: Same test at 11:30 AM near building on east side.

Design No. 290 was readable at 94 feet.

Design 296L was readable at 84 feet.

Design 296 was readable at 73 feet.

SUMMARY

DESIGN

Design No. 296 and Design No. 296L are equally good in design quality.

Design No. 290 is second best in design quality.

VISIBILITY

Design No. 296 and Design No. 296L are best in visibility.

Design No. 290 has second best visibility.'

READABILITY

Design No. 290 has best readability.

Design No. 296L has the second best readability.

Design No. 296 has the poorest readability.

Designs No. 299 and 295 are poor in design and in visibility although they are as good as No. 296L in readability.

CONCLUSION

Design No. 296L is best in design, best in visibility and second best in readability.

Swatches for Red and Blue Colors are Enclosed.

The recommended red has greater visibility than the red on Design Nos. 296 or 296L, and has greater visibility than any other red.

The blue is the color that should be used for printed matter only, in advertising, packaging, letterheads, etc. The blue on Design No. 296 has greater visibility than any other blue.

APPENDIX

The following are articles in which automobile trends were predicted more than a year before publication of this book!

From *THE KANSAS CITY TIMES*, April 19, 1958.

Sputniks altered American attitudes about such things as motor cars and women's clothes, Louis Cheskin, Chicago, Director of the Color Research Institute, said here yesterday at the ninth district convention of The Advertising Federation of America.

"The discovery that while we are fussing with useless decorations the Russians are making satellites and rockets had a profound psychological effect on almost every American," Cheskin said.

"Studies reveal that people who only a year ago were attracted by frills now react unfavorably to functionless objects. Our recent tests show that the American public now wants simple cars, minus elaborate trim; large cars or small ones, whatever the need, but cars that are simple and functional in design.

"The chemise or sack dress is an attempt, in my opinion a perverted one, to meet the sudden demand for simplicity. The fashion industry has been more sensitive to the public wants or needs than the automotive industry.

"Small American cars and small imported cars are in demand. The luxury cars are being bought. The middle priced cars remain, on dealers' floors. I see signs of a revolt against middle class identification... We should not make the mistake of considering the drastic change in the attitudes of Americans toward cars as merely the problem of the car industry."

From *TIME*, April 21,1958.

The U.S. consumer has done a complete and almost unnoticed turnabout in taste recently. So Researcher Louis Cheskin, Director of Chicago's Color Research Institute, this week told the Advertising Federation of America. Said Cheskin: The entire attitude of the American people towards "ostentatious ornamentation" has changed drastically in the last few months, especially in cars. "As recently as last year, our tests showed that people reacted favorably to elaborate ornamentation, gaudy color combinations and chrome trim on cars and other steel products. The recent studies show that people are reacting unfavorably to such functionless frills."

What will sell cars in the future? Says Researcher Cheskin: "The sober look, the dignified form, the basically functional gadget, the single color or truly two-tone color. Useless gadgets do not appeal to the 1958 shoppers and will appeal to the 1959 and 1960 shoppers even less. The jukebox effect will disappear. Elaborate ornamentation of chrome and multiple colors will be discarded. Finally, consumers are also beginning to resent forced obsolescence. When yearly fashions were limited to women's apparel, there was almost universal acceptance. The public did not resist the yearly car design changes. Then other hardgoods makers began planned obsolescence. Perhaps this has broken the camel's back. Now the consumer is in revolt."

From *NEWSWEEK*, April 28,1958.

From Los Angeles's Mayor Norris Poulson came criticism of the "Big, big, flashy, chrome-encrusted, multi-powered car." Harvard economist Sumner H. Slichter partly blamed "the weird collection of headlights, fins, tails, wings, etc." for the recession. And such a latter-day seer as Chicago's Motivational Researcher Louis Cheskin told the automen "to take a good look at the recent psychological change in the American people to discover the cure for their lagging sales. Our studies indicate that simplicity should characterize auto design."

Sputnik caused it all, says Cheskin soberly. "The discovery that while we were fussing with useless decorations the Russians were making satellites and intercontinental rockets has had a profound psychological effect on almost every American."

From *STEEL, The Metalworking Weekly*, April 28,1958.

WHAT DO CAR BUYERS WANT?

LET'S FIND OUT—Since styling seems to count, Louis Cheskin, Director, Color Research Institute, Chicago, suggests motivational research might help automakers discover what people want in time to change designs or at least to plan marketing campaigns playing up each car's strong points.

Motivational research supposedly finds out what people subconsciously want instead of what they say they want. Mr. Cheskin calls it "unconscious testing." He says: "Last year our tests showed people reacted favorably to elaborate ornamentation, gaudy color combinations, and intricate chrome trim."

"But our studies show people who were attracted by frills a year ago now react unfavorably to functionless objects. Flamboyant fins and chrome trim don't excite the 1958 shopper and will appeal even less to the 1959 and 1960 buyers."

STUDIES REVEAL—Using such testing methods, Mr. Cheskin finds Ford's Thunder bird ranks first in styling appeal and Lincoln second. Chevrolet and Oldsmobile are fairly high; Buick and Pontiac are on the bottom part of the list stylewise.

T-Bird and Lincoln styling features less chrome and more utilitarianism. Pontiac and Buick approach elaborate ornamentation Mr. Cheskin claims buyers no longer want. Sales and production figures seem to substantiate his theory: Ford says it has built

10,000 four-passenger Thunderbirds and that dealers have more than 10,000 unfilled orders.

NOT NAPPING—Automakers are not unaware of Mr. Cheskin's conclusions. Says Harley J. Earl, GM's styling vice president: "In past surveys estimates were that 15 per cent of the people wanted less chrome and 85 per cent want chrome as we had it. This percentage has dropped to 50-50, and we're deleting chrome as rapidly as possible."

NO HELP—No matter how much motivational research reveals about people's real wants, it still won't help design cars that won't appear for two more years. At best it may decrease the magnitude of errors.

Mr. Cheskin suggests motivational tests on parts such as grilles, light assemblies, and quarter panels could be conducted in advance without tipping off new model plans. Edsel's story might have been different if such tests had been run before finalizing designs.

Reports Mr. Cheskin: "In an association test we made as soon as the Edsel appeared, respondents were asked to associate the car image with one of five years—1935, 1940, 1945, 1950, 1955. The greatest number associated it with 1935." This isn't quite the youthful, futuristic appeal Edsel aimed for.

LOOK AHEAD—Over a period, Mr. Cheskin believes, producers can build up a backlog of test surveys which point out trends with some accuracy. "Our studies show that in the next few years we should expect customer resistance to frills. We have some evidence it may be advisable for carmakers to change styling every three years, co-ordinating style changes with product improvement. Cars with the greatest simplicity of design will be in greatest demand."

From *FORTUNE*, May 1958.

The Perennial Rebellion

Are American consumers really fed up with chrome, frills, and gewgaws? Many observers have been saying so lately. One of them,

Chicago motivation researcher Louis Cheskin, claims he can prove it. "As recently as last year," says Cheskin, "our tests showed that people reacted favorably to elaborate ornamentation, gaudy color combinations, and elaborate chrome trim on cars and other steel products . . . Recent studies show that people are reacting unfavorably to such ostentatious ornamentation . . . Now the consumer is in revolt."

. . . While people are heralding the consumers' revolt against forced obsolescence, women are throwing away last year's dresses and getting into sacks (which, by the way, Mr. Cheskin terms "a perverted attempt to meet the sudden demand for simplicity").

INDEX

www.ingramcontent.com/pod-product-compliance
Lightning Source LLC
Chambersburg PA
CBHW020527270326
41927CB00006B/477